# Woman of Valor

# woman
## *of* valor

## Lihi Lapid

gefen publishing house
בית הוצאה לאור
JERUSALEM ◆ NEW YORK    Est. 1981

Cover Design: Benjie Herskowitz, Etc. Studios
Typesetting: Irit Nachum


ISBN: 978-965-229-640-5

1 3 5 7 9 8 6 4 2


Gefen Publishing House Ltd.
6 Hatzvi Street
Jerusalem 94386, Israel
972-2-538-0247
orders@gefenpublishing.com

Gefen Books
11 Edison Place
Springfield, NJ 07081
516-593-1234
orders@gefenpublishing.com

**www.gefenpublishing.com**

Printed in Israel

Library of Congress Cataloging-in-Publication Data

Lapid, Lihie.
[Eshet Chayil. English]
Woman of valor / Lihi Lapid.
pages cm
Originally published by Kineret : Zemorah-Bitan, in Hebrew as Eshet Chayil.
Includes bibliographical references and index.
ISBN 978-965-229-640-5 (alk. paper)
I. Title.
PJ5055.29.A646513E84 2013
892.4'37—dc23

# 1

*It is not good that the man should be alone...*

(Genesis 2:18)

I sat at night, in my empty house, and after so many years of longing for a moment of quiet for myself, I realized that I hated this silence. Suddenly I knew that what I'd thought I wanted wasn't what I really wanted. I understood that I was so preoccupied with sorrow and anger that I wasn't looking at all the good things that I *did* have. I had erased them. In this moment of clarity I suddenly understood a number of things.

I have to stop wasting and sacrificing my life on the altar of small details. I have to separate between what is important and what isn't. To let go. Because you can't control everything anyway. I won't be able to save my daughter, even if I devote all my time to her – my entire life, all my energies, all of myself. Because sometimes you just can't save someone. I have to stop being angry about what was, agonizing over the past and worrying about the future, because whatever will be, will be. I have to remember that the here and now is also important, and I have to enjoy it. Because *now* will never come again.

This moment can be good. And this one good moment plus another one is what happiness is made of. Because happiness is something that suddenly emerges, illuminating the sky for one second, for one moment, and then it passes. It's so easy to miss them, those tiny moments of happiness. For too many years, I had let them pass without even noticing them. Without even stopping to rejoice in them.

And for the first time I thought about what I wanted. Not what I wanted from other people – not what I wanted others to do, to be, to give me – but what I wanted from myself. And I wanted so many things. Too many things. I knew it wouldn't be easy, that I would have to change myself. But considering the fact that I hadn't smiled for so long, that years had passed since I had last laughed, and that I had pretty much ruined my life, I didn't really have anything to lose.

Dear Lihi,

I'm 32 years old and single. Educated, employed, and making an honest living; attractive, healthy, thank God, and happy with my life. God in heaven and my heart know how much I yearn and long, after so many frustrating dates, to meet *the one*. How I long to stand, deliriously happy, with my love, my partner, and vow eternal love; how I long to start a glorious family of my own, to hold my firstborn in my arms and weep with elation. Yet, unfortunately, my private pain has become public knowledge to all those concerned. "Don't you want to get married already?" "How come you haven't gotten married yet?" they hurl at me in accusatory tones. "Why do you reject everyone?" They label me, without having any idea whether I actually do the rejecting, or perhaps I'm the one being rejected. One kind soul even berated me for

the aging of my ova. I cried for two days. I've
had enough! They should just stop.

Sharon

I thought of the first time we met. The sun was rising and the city
behind us emitted the first sounds of morning. We rose from the
reclining deck chairs on the empty beach, and he asked me what
he had to do in order to see me again. I found a piece of paper,
wrote my phone number on it, gave it to him, and said that I'd be
very pleased if he called. He laughed and told me to remember
that I was the one who made the first move.

The few friends I told about him, who had only my best
interests at heart, immediately summoned expressions of concern
and hastily explained to me that there was no future here, and
that at my age – not even twenty – it was foolish to get into a
relationship with a man who was divorced and had a child. But
I wasn't thinking that far into the future. He was interesting,
different, and he made me laugh. It was enough for me to fall
in love. Two and a half years after that sunrise, he went away
for several days, and I missed him so much that the minute he
showed up with his suitcases, I ran to him and asked him if he
wanted to marry me.

Hi, Lihi,

Many thanks for that moisturizer you recommended.
Several friends of mine and I bought the product
and our skins are glowing and looking better
than ever. Now all we need is to hear your
recommendations as to the type of men we should
marry, so if there's any preference whatsoever,
do tell.

Rina

He agreed to marry me. My mother told me that getting married so young was a mistake, but I was twenty-two and a half, and felt ready and mature enough to start real life. I loved him and wanted a commitment. I wanted to commit to him and him to me. To do the right thing. For him to be my husband and me to be his wife. I was prepared to move on to the next stage.

I never had any fantasies concerning event planning, and the wedding itself wasn't important to me at all. So we decided on a small ceremony in a restaurant. I hadn't worn a dress since third grade, and my hair had been short since fifth grade; I never wore makeup, and I wasn't about to make an issue now about what to wear. One day, I went out and bought a white dress. As far as I was concerned, this was where the preparations for the big day ended.

Two days before the wedding, his parents brought me, as a gift, a small, delicate gold watch. That same day, my mother appeared with a gift of her own: a massive silver necklace. His parents and mine expected me to wear their gifts at the wedding. Even a girl like me, clueless and lacking any passion whatsoever concerning anything to do with fashion, could see that these two pieces couldn't be worn together in any way.

On the day of my wedding, in the afternoon, we went, my man and I, down the steps of our rented apartment and into our car. It was all so ordinary and so routine, except for one thing: I was dressed up in a long dress made of a rich and wonderful cream-colored material, and for the first time in my life, I looked like a woman.

I got married wearing the large silver necklace that my parents gave me and the small gold watch that his parents gave me. Even though they didn't go together.

I am 25 years old, and perhaps, according to your standards, I'm still young. However, as an Orthodox woman, whose girlfriends were all married at the ages of 19 or 20 and already have children, I'm no longer considered young. The only "merchandise" left at this age is people on the fringes, or as we call them, the riffraff. When I heard that a good friend was pregnant for the third time, I thought that all was lost for me. But I decided that I wouldn't compromise, even if I was still alone.

Suddenly, one month ago, he appeared. He was there, all the time, right under my nose, and I had no idea. It's been a month already and I'm walking around with a smile smeared all over my face, understanding that I haven't missed a thing, and that it was worth waiting.

Just when I thought that it wouldn't happen to me and the pressure from home and from every direction had reached a peak, this angel appeared. The strangest thing about this entire story is that he's not religious, and we're slowly learning to compromise. He'll honor what's important to me and in return, I'll honor him. So, that's it. Now it's my turn. Now it's my turn to love.

Rachel

The princess is dancing at her wedding ball, her long white dress flying with every movement she makes, wrapping her in an aura of purity. She's as beautiful as a princess in a fairy tale, just like she dreamed she would be. She's floating on a cloud of happiness that dulls the pain of the blisters caused by her new shoes, and she's spinning around, celebrating the moment, the pinnacle, the peak, the most important evening of her life, the end of this process, of the questions, the wonder, the hesitancy about this decision that was so difficult to make. The decision to entwine her life, forever and ever, with someone else's life. Through thick and thin. For better or for worse. Of all the people in the world. It took her so long to find him. And him to find her.

She stops for a minute, catches her breath and searches for him among the celebrators, and she sees him somewhere, at the edge of the large ballroom – the prince, swaying drunkenly. *My sweet*, she thinks, *doesn't really know how to drink, which is good*, she says to herself, *and he laughs too much, which is nice, and here are his charming friends surrounding him*, friends who will accompany them forever and ever, and no, she won't ask what happened at the bachelor party because she knows that he loves her. And he knows that she loves him.

The princess is so happy – everyone keeps telling her that she's so beautiful and glowing – she forgets everything that happened before this evening, all the arguments between his parents and hers, that fight they had, he and she, when they were torn between former loyalties to the families from which each of them came and their new commitment to each other, and the indecision between the purple napkins that she wanted and the pink ones that his mother wanted. Another waiter passes by, crossing the room with a tray laden with dirty dishes, and for a second, she lands with a crash from her cloud, petrified. For a moment it seems to her as though she's no more than an actress in some end-of-the-year school play, hiding the fact that she's not who everyone thinks she is, and that she actually still feels like a little girl, that she's afraid, that he's not really a man but just a young prince who has just started his life, and that there's no chance that the wedding gifts they'll receive will cover the expenses for this evening, which have unintentionally swelled to monstrous proportions. She doesn't really understand how it happened. They had promised themselves a small, modest event, and now she's wearing a dress that costs more than all the clothes she has ever bought in her life.

She inhales deeply, observing all the aunts and uncles eating, and all the strangers scrutinizing her. Her parents are approaching, their chests puffed out with pride. They hug her, and the photographer captures them with his flash, the bride and her parents, and she hastily summons a smile. Today she's the star of the evening. Someone pulls her onto the dance floor, and again she's spinning on a cloud somewhere. *Mazal tov*, congratulations. From the other side of the room the prince smiles at her, and she smiles back at him. She loves him so much, and she knows that he loves her deeply, and that they're going to be happy together. They're a wonderful couple.

# 2

*And she became his wife; and he loved her...*

(Genesis 24:67)

One day, I received a phone call from the newspaper where I worked as a photographer. They asked me if I wanted to fly to Rwanda the next day. Members of the Hutu tribe had perpetrated a horrendous massacre against members of the Tutsi tribe. Ever since I had started taking pictures, somewhere around the age of sixteen, this had been my dream: to be a real press photographer sent to the battlefield. I didn't hesitate for a minute. I said yes and started packing. The next morning, together with the soldiers, I boarded a military plane that contained an entire hospital in its belly.

It was easy to discern between them, between the Hutu and the Tutsi. The Tutsi were tall and thin, and the Hutu were short and husky. Thousands of lost, orphaned children, naked and famished, wandered shell-shocked among the tall and short tribe members. The old people died from hunger on the side of the road, between rows of bodies wrapped in wool blankets, secured with ropes. I tried to hide behind the camera, struggling to maintain sanity in the presence of all the inconceivable pain and sorrow, death, helplessness, and doom.

At one point, through the fog I had wrapped around myself, I heard the crying of a little boy. I approached him. He was so small, no more than two years old. He sat on a rock and cried. We asked the people in the area whose boy he was. Without looking at us, they said that they didn't know. "How long has he been here?" we asked. "Two days," they answered. "Did you give him anything to drink, to eat?" we asked, and I had to stop myself from screaming at these people, who had lost everything they had, including their compassion. No, they hadn't given him anything, because they didn't know him.

We took him to the camp that was a gathering point for the orphaned children; I told the woman in charge that I wanted to take him with me. I even called home and told my man that I was bringing a child. For several seconds, silence descended on the other side of the line. Then, he told me that he'd stand by my side no matter what I decided. But they wouldn't let me. "Perhaps his mother will return," said the people in charge of the orphans' camp, while they weighed him on cattle scales.

Like everyone who was there, I returned from Rwanda a different person. Things that had excited me before lost their significance. Photography, which up until that day had seemed to me the most significant and most essential thing in the world, and for more than a decade was what actually defined me, suddenly became to me nothing more than work. The enthusiasm that had burned within me dimmed. It was no longer exciting. I had already taken a bite out of the career apple. I had flirted with the snake of success; I had even had a solo show in a museum. It's true that I hadn't touched all the heights that I had meant to reach, but I felt satisfied with what I'd achieved. Now, I wanted something else. Something that would truly fill me, that would be important and real. Maybe my age had started affecting me. I knew what my next assignment was.

I always knew that I was one of those girls who took her time. I started studying for my degree only at the age of 30, and now, I'm facing a wedding, and I'm terrified! I'm still a student and at my "old" age, I still don't have a career, and I have no idea if I'll ever have one, because I really want kids, and it goes without saying that I can't really wait, which means that there's already no chance of going out and finding a career, because childrearing requires time, and I want to give it time, and treat it seriously, but everything looms so big and threatening.

Suddenly, I have to consider someone else's wishes, and if, until now, I worked as a bartender in dark pubs and clubs, now I'll have to find another job, because my man doesn't really like the fact that his girlfriend is working in shady places. It's understandable. And it's not.

Now, I also have to consider my man's tight-knit, united family. And the thoughts: Will I succeed; will I fail; will I be a good wife, a good friend, a good mother? What will happen? What's the method? How does it work? And where, in this entire mess, do our private, personal dreams enter? Where do they disappear? Suddenly, I have a feeling that when you get married, something stops and you enter a routine of commitment and obligation. Children, mortgage, and husband: we have to try to please them all. Isn't that true? Oh, I'm so confused...tell me, is it natural? Are there others like me? Am I alone?

Nava

The prince and princess's love story isn't so thrilling that a fairy tale was written about them. They weren't forced to cross mountains and rivers in order to be together, nor did they have to slay dragons or witches, and an evil queen didn't even interfere with their love. Some stories are more romantic: Romeo and Juliet, Julia Roberts and Richard Gere. Some stories are also less romantic: online matchmaking sites, dates set up by an aunt. Even though their love story isn't unique, and poems haven't been written about it, they certainly aren't just another couple. They are two charming young people, full of potential. Each of them separately and both of them together. Two young people who have done all the right things, and who now face the beginning of life with all the odds in their favor.

Two days after the wedding, they get up and go to work. The prince is slightly older than the princess. That's how it usually is, with regular mortals as well as with royalty. The prince earns slightly more, because he has a bit more seniority at his workplace than she does at hers. They don't make an issue out of it. The prince never makes her feel as though he is more important because he earns more. Neither does she feel as though she is less important because of that. Money isn't an issue for them anyway; they don't need much of it. They have each other, and they are full of expectations for the great future. They know that they will have to work hard, and they don't have a problem with that, because they are two diligent people.

They start devoting themselves to building their shared future. They know that they can do it. They also know that they can always count on each other. For the prince and the princess are, above all, true friends for life. It's obvious that they'll help each other, come hell or high water, and even while cleaning their apartment, the rent for which, incidentally, eats up half of their combined salary.

Time goes by. He's worked hard and he's been promoted. She's also succeeding pretty well. Slowly, things are starting to come together. They even buy a new refrigerator. Just thirty-six monthly payments. Occasionally, the prince brings her flowers on Friday, and she pampers him one day by cooking a dish that he loves, a recipe from his mother. One day she decides to invite some friends for a real dinner. For three days she is under an enormous amount of pressure but in the end it is wonderful and everyone compliments her.

After some time, they start feeling that itch. They feel it's time to move forward to the next stage. They also start to hear the ticking. The ticking of the clock. The princess hears it before the prince, and it bothers her a bit more, but the prince also realizes that the time has come. It's the next logical step. The love is there, the friendship is there, and there's even a little savings plan that will one day be a big savings plan, and now they have to make all this potential into reality. They start talking about a child. After all, there's one goal to this entire business, which is to bring into the world tiny princesses and princes who will later wander the world with noses or eyes just like theirs. Preferably the prince's eyes and the princess's nose. And if not, no big deal. Nowadays, plastic surgery is an option.

# 3

## *Be fruitful, and multiply, and replenish the earth...*

### (Genesis 1:28)

The man I married was a father before he met me. His fatherhood was one of the most significant things about who he was, and I loved and admired him for it. As time went on, I was further exposed to the force of this love, this pure love, the love of a parent for his child, and I tried to be part of that love, to be Daddy's good wife. Now, I wanted to feel it as well. To feel this thing, this love I had heard so much about and seen close up. My return from Rwanda, which precipitated my disillusionment with photography, left me with a feeling that something was missing, and I felt that this was what could fill the emptiness, the gaping void within me.

And from that moment, nothing else interested me. Only that. Doing the most important thing: bringing a child into the world and being a mother. To touch those endless skies, that peak, to feel that enormous experience. I'd still have time to climb up the ladder of success later on; I'd still have time to try to scratch the earth and leave my mark. All of these things could wait. Okay, I told myself, I'm doing it. That's it. I'm at the age to jump through the hoop, even if it's a bit scary –terrifying, actually – but I have to take a deep breath and do it. There's no point in waiting anymore. I have to do it and get it over with. Just like a bungee jump. You close your eyes and leap.

Another routine checkup at the gynecologist. I was three months pregnant. It was also my third pregnancy. The first two had ended in failure. Nothing special; they just fell into the statistics that no one ever told me about. I fell apart those first two times, certain that I was infertile, that I'd never hold a child of my own in my arms. And now, once again, that look on the dear doctor's face, his smile faltering. I stopped breathing. When he said, "Listen," I knew that it wasn't going to be good news, and I tried not to cry, cursing myself for having come alone. I'd come by myself because I didn't want to be a burden and felt uncomfortable calling my man each time. I could do everything independently and I didn't need anyone to hold my hand. I was strong. I was self-sufficient.

But I did need someone to hold my hand. Desperately. And like the moron that I was, I hadn't even told him that I had a checkup, and I'd just stopped in at the doctor on my way somewhere else. The good doctor saw that I was on the verge of tears, and he said that everything was okay, just some bleeding that was bothering him, and that he wanted me to lie down. I was so overjoyed that I wanted to hug him. Nevertheless, tears coursed down my face, and I promised to rest. Then he said that I had to rest a lot. So I asked for how long, and he said several weeks.

Dear Lihi,

Many times, when you write about your children, I cry. I'm not a depressive type – quite the opposite. I'm usually happy. The thing is that

I've been trying to get pregnant for the last two years, with no success, and I'm not alone in this. We all know what menstrual pains are, but we don't know how painful our menstruation is when we don't want it to arrive. Only someone in a situation similar to mine can understand. I am writing to you and hoping that you'll print these words for the sake of all those kind souls, the majority of them women, who know you for one year, five years, and sometimes only five minutes and ask: "Don't you want kids? Why? Because of the money?"

People find so many ways to nose their way into our wombs and twist the knife just a little bit more. I want them to know that it doesn't really demonstrate friendliness or interest. Whether we've decided that we don't want children, or that we have no way to sustain a child, or we're having fertility issues, it's simply nobody's business. Stop with this nosiness. Please stop. You're hurting us terribly.

Shoshana

The prince and the princess announce to everyone, with great festivity and excitement, that they're pregnant. She and he are pregnant. Both. And they're not afraid. Yes, they already know about morning sickness; they've heard in detail about all the symptoms. So many aunts and other elderly women have tried to scare them, telling them that the princess should rest a bit, slow down. Sometimes, even young mothers holding wipes in one hand join the congregation of alarmists and tell them that they have no idea what is yet ahead of them: the vomiting, the nauseating sickness, the distorted body, the swollen feet – and don't forget to put your feet up to prevent varicose veins – but all that doesn't scare them. They grasp each other's hands and smile at everyone, well aware that it won't happen to them, because they're together and they'll support each other, and nowadays things are different, and she isn't spoiled, even though she is a princess. Besides, pregnancy isn't a sickness.

The princess, who before her pregnancy had wandered the globe and hung out in remote locations, who studied, worked, moved mountains, and headed projects, isn't alarmed. She isn't so easily alarmed. She's strong. She's read; she's heard; she knows that it's up to her what kind of attitude she'll have. She knows that she's going to approach this with love and joy, entirely willing and prepared, and that's how she'll get through it. She's not going to become one of those fat women who walk like a duck. Not her. She's going to have a lovely pregnancy, like young women have nowadays, and she'll continue everything as usual. She's going to continue dancing, and rejoicing, and will float lightly and proudly with her belly protruding, so that everyone will look at her and burst with envy. Because the princess knows she is embarking on the biggest journey of them all. She is going to complete the perfect picture of her life.

■ ■ ■

I lay in my bed; a week passed, and then another. From a girl zooming around independently on a motor scooter, with a job, a studio, an assistant who came in every day after surfing the waves – and if the waves were good he wouldn't come in at all, and I couldn't get mad at him – I had turned into a breeding tank that had to ponder every movement, to lie down as much as possible, and do as little as possible. I remained horizontal for another week, and another week, staring at the television, becoming addicted to daily installments of the life story of Antonella, an orphaned housekeeper who's in love with the son of the landlord. I became stupid, and saw how all the things once important to me were growing further and further away from me, fading, and I didn't care at all. Because I wanted a child. That was the only thing on my mind, the only thing I cared about. I wanted a child. I wanted it more than anything; I wanted it like someone who couldn't have it wants it. Madly.

So I lay in bed for six months, as women do when they're going through a high-risk pregnancy. I lay in bed and gained fifty pounds and three chins in front of my soap opera. It really was the most wonderful thing that had ever happened to me. And no, it wasn't a sickness. Of course, there were always those who said it was terribly sexy. Right, sexy, no doubt about that. I was a sexy, stupid hippo, who lay in bed and was supposed to glow with joy and feel as though I was doing the most wonderful and important thing in the world.

I'm in my early thirties, and I know that it's not going to be like it is in the commercials. Yeah, yeah, children are wonderful. However, I was many things before them and I know all those things are going to have to wait their turn on the sidelines. When I wake up in the middle of the night, vomiting, with heartburn, and I have to pee and eat, we both remember the sentence "Pregnancy isn't a sickness" and laugh tiredly. I am completely exhausted and it's only the first trimester of the pregnancy. Anyway, we've gone

through massive bonding processes so we can feel
as though all this is right, and wonderful, and
instinctive.

You said that kids can be born ugly, and I
wanted to thank you for saying it because no one
is willing to admit this fact. I was told that
"when it's yours, you won't see things that way."
I doubt it. Not a lot of people say it as it is.
And although it may not be comforting, it still
helps me feel less lonely. Thank you.

Shira

The prince and the princess go together to childbirth education class, and when they sit there, he hugs her and strokes her belly. They hear all the explanations and decide to do it naturally. They want the birth to be as natural and genuine as possible and the experience to be perfect. The course instructor says that it depends on them only. On their willpower. The strong princess knows that she wants it natural; they both want it, and besides, she knows that the prince will be there with her. He'll help her. He won't wait outside like his father did. He'll be there with her, breathe with her, hold her hand, massage her back. They will arrive at the delivery room prepared and ready for the greatest experience of all. He knows what to do. He even sat for one whole evening and chose what music he'd play for her in the delivery room – all the songs that she loves best.

Occasionally, during the night, the princess wakes up in alarm. She's afraid of the birth. She recalls all sorts of scary stories, and she's concerned. She, who until this pregnancy didn't even know that her body has other uses apart from finding it a flattering item to wear, dieting it, or finding its G-spot, is now encased in a body with a life of its own. A life that has nothing to do with her. Her breasts grow to enormous dimensions, tears erupt from her suddenly without control, and this feeling of nausea – which she was told would pass in a minute – did pass, but then other things replaced it: she has heartburn, and her pretty legs have swollen up, and pimples have covered her entire face, and her hair has thinned, and then there are her nerves, which are completely frayed.

She wakes the prince, and he strokes her – her sweet prince – and soothes her. "You're wonderful," he says. "You were never more beautiful," he whispers, and he'll be there with her during the birth, he'll protect her, and she has nothing to worry about because everything will be just wonderful. And she calms down.

# 4

*As a woman with child, that draweth near
the time of her delivery, is in pain,
and crieth out in her pangs...*

(Isaiah 26:17)

The big moment finally arrives. The prince and the princess go together to give birth. The princess doesn't understand why it's so complicated, why it's so painful, why it isn't proceeding smoothly and calmly like they were told in the course, why all the breathing isn't helping. Okay, it's true that she *is* trying to push a watermelon out of a relatively small hole in her body, but the instructor said that it wouldn't be hard if she'd just make the effort... Suddenly, everyone surrounding her panics and calls the doctor even though she begs them not to, just like she was told in the course where she was told not to give in. The doctor insists that the baby is stuck and that there's no other choice.

She doesn't understand why this isn't working out like she wanted it to. What's the big deal? So many women have done it before – billions of women – and nowadays it's easier, we know more. Once, women gave birth without all the anesthesia and the medication and the paraphernalia that we have today. She's already blurry from all this pain, and the voices around her are beginning to fade away. All she hears is the monitor beeping and the thumping of a tiny heart, which sounds like horses galloping, a gallop growing slower and slower, and she understands that the little heart of the little creature within her is slowing down and suddenly she recalls that once women died during childbirth. Many women and babies died.

But what does that have to do with what's happening now? She tries not to think about it and reminds herself of what the course instructor said, about her being responsible, and that it has everything to do with what she wants, with her inner strength. The instructor told them about women giving birth in the hot tub, at home, and the baby slipped out of them in fifteen minutes, and while they're giving birth, they're also dancing the samba, and if only she had the guts, she'd give birth to the baby at home, easy as pie, but she's a pathetic coward – that's how she feels about insisting on going to the hospital, about panicking at the last minute, during the last wave of pain. She's forgotten all her promises, and her decisions, and even though the prince tries to remind her that they decided on natural childbirth, without epidural, in the end she's taken to the operating room and has a C-section.

■ ■ ■

I pushed and pushed and there, the midwife said, the head is crowning, just a little more, a bit more; my man held my hand and I pushed a bit more, even though I no longer had the strength, and suddenly he was out. That was it. I did it. And it actually wasn't that awful; as a matter of fact, it was even wonderful. I was so grateful for all the drugs that they shoved at me and I couldn't believe that I'd really done it. I was in seventh heaven. And they put my baby on me.

Even though my purse was jammed with his ultrasound pictures, I was so surprised. Surprised that until several minutes ago, I really did have a child inside that enormous belly. A real child. I mean, almost a real child. He was much smaller, dirtier, shrunken, and bluer than I thought he'd be, but now he was lying on me, this tiny boy, and he was the most amazing thing in the world. And he had everything, knock on wood, and everything was in its rightful place. He was the sweetest baby to ever leave his mother's belly. A magical boy.

I fell in love with him like I never imagined that I could. I never imagined that this love would sweep me away, shake me, capture me, take me from myself, and put me in another place.

I was happy. And proud.

Then they took him to wash him and said that they'd return him in a minute, and they moved me to the recovery room. I lay there alone, my entire body still trembling from the effort, and all I wanted was for them to bring him back to me, so I could look at him for another minute, at that tiny wonder, and I couldn't even talk. I thought about how happy I was. And suddenly I realized that I was also terribly afraid. Actually, I was terrified.

Nevertheless, I told everyone that I was happy.

Because that's what you're supposed to say.

So I smiled at everyone, even though I was frightened. Here's this little creature who emerged from me just today, and in no time I'll be sent home with him, still bleeding and bruised, to take care of him. To tend to him and all his needs. To understand him. "Nurse, can you please explain to me again how to put my nipple in his mouth?" Why hadn't I been told that breast-feeding is so complicated and painful? Why couldn't he hold on to the nipple? Without the diaper he looked so small and fragile, and beyond the problem of this little mouth that just couldn't get a hold of my nipple, I was in a heavy fog.

From the faint voices that reached me, I understood that everyone around me had started organizing things in preparation for the brit. They were sending out invitations and they asked me if I wanted meat or dairy, and I was so tired that I didn't care. Everything is fine by me, I said, and I tried to smile but I was in so much pain and my hospital gown had the entire whatchamacallit open in the back, and I had stitches and the doctor said he made a special effort when he sewed them and that they came out very nice, and even a nurse and a medical student who just happened to be passing by in the corridor were impressed and said that the stitches were really nice, and I immediately tried to close my legs but it burned so badly; will someone please cover me up, dammit; thanks for the *mazal tov*, and no, no need to visit; you shouldn't have come; thanks for the lovely flowers; and after every pee I had to wash, and my mother was asking me what color tablecloths I wanted for the dinner after the circumcision ceremony and I didn't want any circumcision ceremony.

I didn't want anything. I just wanted everyone to get out of my face for one minute, to take away their chocolates and smiles, and questions about how did it go, and how much does he weigh, and who does he look like, Mommy or Daddy. Because I was choking and I was terrified. I loved him so much; I just needed everyone to give me one minute by myself.

And I didn't have one minute.

Dear Lihi,

Congratulations. My friend just gave birth for the third time. Laden with sweets and gifts,

I walked into her room in the maternity ward, full of expectations and excitement. Yet, when I opened the door, I found a terrified woman staring at a screaming baby asking, "What do I do with it?" ("It" being the baby.) I wasn't sure what to do, but I didn't want to raise the tension level in the room so I recalled that this was a stage in which babies were in one of three possible states: sleeping, eating, and diaper changing. Since sleep wasn't relevant, I suggested we check the eating or diaper-changing options.

Imagine this, two adult women, experienced mothers, standing helpless before six pounds, nine ounces of screaming sweetness. A situation that did not bring to mind, in any way, a commercial for baby formulas. The new mother did not look like the flat-bellied and meticulously made-up model who was shedding a tear of happiness as she breast-fed for the first time, and I didn't portray the supportive friend, reaching serenely for the baby.

Mothers are supposed to feel total and immediate love for their children. There is an expectation that the mythic bonding will occur immediately, and every mother will feel a profound love for her baby and will be guided by this special feeling while tending to her newborn. But in all actuality, many women need time to form a relationship with their babies.

Yael

The princess and prince leave the hospital with their little heir, and now they're home. The princess is terribly tired, but she doesn't care; she's happy. She waited for this for so long, to be with him already, to get to know him, and now she has the time just for that. Just for him. Now she's on maternity leave; she doesn't have to work, and all she has to do is take care of the baby. No big deal. She's done things much more complicated, and she can certainly take care of this tiny thing, who needs only to eat, sleep, and have his diaper changed every three or four hours, like a simple cycle, with a daily bath. All he needs is right here in her breasts, so there's no problem.

It's true that sometimes he cries and she doesn't understand why, or what he wants, and sometimes he really screams, and her stitches hurt her so, and she no longer knows if he's hungry or tired, and when was the last time she fed him, and suddenly she has too much milk and it's painful, and her nipples are bruised and bleeding and she doesn't remember from which breast she last nursed him, because she lives in these short cycles, sleeps for thirty minutes and then gets up. She's completely disoriented and can't control these thoughts that are running back and forth through her head, and sometimes she almost cries, but tries not to, because she knows that it's only her raging hormones, because she's so happy; she's so content. This is what she wanted more than anything else in the world, and she's really trying to get used to living without sleep, to recover from the stitches, and her body is exhausted.

Every hour feels like a week. Guests arrive to congratulate her and they want to see the little wonder, and there she is, sitting in front of them and smiling with her lacerated nipples, with a painful abundance of milk, and she doesn't understand why it's so hard for her. Because she was looking forward to this. To the real thing. To this pleasure. And she feels as though it's wrong that she isn't only happy and delighted. She takes a deep breath, and even though she's exhausted, and her body isn't behaving and feeling like she expected it to, she knows that she's happy. That she's touching the real thing.

It's just a little tiring.

And a little difficult.

Before the birth, the princess asked the Queen Mother, her prince's mother, how they managed things in the past. The queen told her that after she gave birth, she lay in bed for six weeks. It was customary. And her mother and the king's mother were with her and they did everything. Food. Diaper changing. Housework. The princess thought to herself that back then, things were different. Today it's impossible. She can't even think of having the queen suddenly move in with them for several weeks. And it goes without saying that the prince would never agree to have her mother move in with them. Both the queen and her mother offer to drop by and help, but the princess just smiles, thanks them prettily, and says, "It's okay, I'm okay, we're okay, we'll manage." She and the prince.

The princess thinks about how very young the queen was when she gave birth, and she just wasn't ready. She, the princess, is so ready; she's more than prepared, and besides, she knows the king. He's from a different generation. There's no doubt that the king didn't help the queen. Her prince isn't like those old-fashioned men. He's the new man – the man in touch with himself, who has waited for this moment, for this baby, to take care of him and be with him, just as much as she waited for it, and he even takes some time off to help her.

She's sure that the king didn't take any time off.

I wanted to tell you that on Tuesday, I gave
birth to my child, and that all around me, there
are these "kind" people who impart advice and
forget that every person has their own way of
doing things, and perhaps because of all the
hormones raging within me, I'm reading and crying
and sympathizing so. I just wanted you to know.

Rebecca

The prince wakes up in the morning, after three days, kisses the
baby, tells the princess that he'll miss them, and goes to work.
Now, more than ever, he feels that he's shouldering a heavy
responsibility, that he has a real role: to provide. That's his role
now. He's the man, and he's in charge of his family, in charge of
bringing bread to the table, because from now on, it's serious, it's
real, and it's no longer just the two of them. Now there's a child.
An heir. There are a lot of expenses, and the layette itself, with the
changing table and the crib and the best stroller that money can
buy, finished all their savings. He knows that there are going to be
many more expenses.

He feels this burden settling on his shoulders, the burden of
honestly providing for his family. He wants to be able to give the
heir the best there is, to open all the doors when the time comes,
and in order to do that, he has to aspire to move up. He knows
that in order to achieve that, he'll have to work longer hours, and
work harder, and give all he has to give, but he doesn't care. He
isn't doing it for himself, but for their future. His family's future.
And he must succeed. He already knows that it isn't easy to
succeed in this modern world, so he has to put his heart and soul
into his work if he wants to lead the race; he has to try to be the

best; to impress, to invest, to concentrate, to stand out, because he's building their future.

And after three days, when he goes to work, he feels different. He can actually feel the load on his shoulders; he feels the weight of the assignment.

And that sums up the difference between the old-fashioned man and the modern one: three days.

■ ■ ■

I stayed alone at home with my baby. Before I gave birth, I was told that with the birth of the baby, my maternal instincts would awaken, and they'd guide me, so that I'd know what to do, so that I'd understand him immediately and know what he needed. But he was born and I didn't discover a sixth sense in me. I didn't turn into someone else; I didn't know more than I'd known before. I was the same person. The same girl, just with a little baby whom she loved terribly, and who needed her terribly, who cried and whose mother didn't always know what he wanted. And I was very, very tired.

So I hid it. I hid the fact that I didn't really feel this endless joy, because I was afraid that people would misunderstand me. Suddenly, all those horror stories about women who didn't want to touch their babies came back to me – crazy women who did such terrifying things to their children – and I knew that I wasn't like that. And I kept quiet, because I was afraid that people would think that I was suffering from postpartum depression. But I knew that I wasn't. I loved my child; I loved this tiny creature like I had never loved anything in this world before, with an intensity that I had never known before. He was everything to me; he filled everything; he was as pure and lovely as a dream. I wasn't depressed. I was just exhausted, spent, confused, and frightened like I'd never been in my life.

Today, I know that there's a name for this feeling. A sweet name for that tiny depression that is caused by a combination of hormones and stress and this completely new thing that we're facing, that rocks us in recurring waves between terrible sadness and enormous joy, and in the end spits us on the shore, leaving us empty and a bit bleary. Or, in short, depressed. It's called "baby blues." I didn't know back then that I had the blues. I only knew that I was scared to death that I wouldn't know how to be a mother, that I wouldn't be a good mother, that I'd make mistakes. I was overwhelmed by the thought that I was just a simple girl who doesn't understand a thing and now has to be someone she doesn't know how to be: a mother.

I tried to remind myself that I was on maternity leave. A wonderful maternity leave. But I didn't feel like I was on a vacation in Thailand; I felt as though I was in prison.

```
I'm sitting here and reading, with an eight-day-
old baby in my arms (yes, today was the brit with
the help of God and David, the mohel), and what
surprises me, each time anew, is how my most
personal and intimate worries and difficulties are
basically everyone's business. My little worries
are those of every mother, wife, and woman. As
special as I am, I'm just like everyone else.
There is something comforting and at the same
time diminishing in this recognition.
Daphna
```

The princess is at home all day with the heir. They have many magical moments together, and she doesn't stop inhaling him, breathing into her that pure and perfect scent. She looks at his tiny hands in wonderment and a friend tells her that she has to cut his nails, but she's afraid to because everything about him is so tiny; she'll ask the prince to cut his nails because he's already scratched himself. The hours pass by and even though she napped for something like half an hour when he slept, she's tired again, and it's already afternoon, and she's simply exhausted, and he's crying again, and she's feeding him again, but it doesn't help. She holds him and presses his belly, like she was told to do; she summons up all her energies, and all her patience, and rocks and swings and looks at the clock.

Evening is approaching and she feels like taking a shower, but she can't leave the heir, so she waits for the prince to arrive already. To take him for a minute. And another fifteen minutes pass. He was supposed to be home by now. And finally, the door opens, and he's standing there, the prince; and instead of throwing everything from his hands, snatching the child away from her, covering him with a million kisses, telling her that she's the bravest princess of all Snow Whites, covering her also with a million kisses, listening to everything she went through today, all the wonderful things as well as the number of times that she cleaned up poop, how and where the heir spit up on her, instead of all that, all the prince wants to do is to sit quietly for one minute and eat something. Because he had a tough day at work.

He wants to talk to her about his day, and she wants to listen and support, like she once did, but she waited so eagerly for him to come home, to get excited by this tiny creature who screamed all day and if not that, to at least hold him for a bit so that she'll be able to take a shower, and perhaps eat something, and talk to someone. After the prince eats a little something that he warmed up in the microwave, he relieves her of the heir, and she goes to take a shower, and later, when he holds the heir in his arms, she sits down and eats a little something. Alone.

# 5

*And the woman took the child, and nursed it.*

(Exodus 2:9)

It was obvious to the prince and princess that they would breast-feed their baby. They read a pile of books, and they know how important it is for their child, for his connection with his mother, for his soul and health. So they breast-feed.

The prince tries to help as much as he can. He even gets up at night, when the heir cries, but as long as she's breast-feeding, the prince can't do much more than bring the heir to her. To her breast, to the only thing that calms his crying. The prince changes his diaper and thinks about how his father definitely never did this, and he is in seventh heaven. He also burps him. And even though he says all the right things, and does all the things that his father didn't do, he begins to feel a bit unnecessary. He suspects that he isn't really helping her, and can't really relieve her. He can't calm down the baby, because this is something that only she can do. Because she's the only one breast-feeding. Because the heir wants and needs only her breasts, and that's the only thing that calms him and puts him to sleep.

Three weeks ago I gave birth to my third son after
a short and difficult pregnancy. I gave birth in

my 27th week to a lovely creature weighing two pounds, seven ounces. He was quickly moved to the premature babies' ward in the hospital and I was released from the hospital after two days, sent home to my older children, to a whirlwind of taking care of my house and husband, numerous trips to the preemie ward, intensive milk expression, and sad nights without the baby. I experienced little moments of joy that grew with every fraction of an ounce that my baby gained. Never in my life did I imagine that half an ounce would make me so happy and jubilant for the entire day, and mostly grateful – grateful that he's okay, that he's breathing, that he's mine.

This experience taught me an important lesson in gratitude. Nothing should be taken for granted or considered obvious. Giving birth to a big, healthy boy at the end of a pregnancy is something that many people do not take for granted. The preemie ward in the hospital is teeming with babies, and the nurses there work so hard, with such devotion and professionalism, standing on their feet for hours, going from child to child and from parent to parent. It's not something that one can take for granted. It deserves much more recognition.

Shirley

And then he choked. Just like that, suddenly, while he was feeding, he drew his head back from my nipple, tried to breathe and couldn't. And in his little face, I saw his big, blue eyes growing wider and wider, and then even wider, and his mouth opening in a desperate attempt to find some oxygen, to breathe, and he wasn't uttering a sound, not a sound, and this silence screamed in my soul, tore me to pieces, and I turned him upside down, and he still didn't breathe, and I stopped breathing too, and pounded on his back, and ran to the faucet, and then I ran in circles inside the apartment, pounding on his back again and again. It seemed to me as though an eternity had passed and amidst this horror and the earsplitting silence, I remembered the upstairs neighbor, a serious young woman with a little girl. Maybe she'd know what to do, because she probably took a first-aid course or something like that, and his blue eyes bulged even more, his mouth wide open, trying to find residues of oxygen, and I was sure that that was it, that with the time gone by he had suffered brain damage, and in another minute I'd lose him, and I ran upstairs, to the neighbor, and on the stairs, probably from all the shaking, something opened up and suddenly he started breathing, and then crying, and I cried with him, and I fell on the floor next to the neighbor's door, crying, unable to calm down; I felt shivers running down my body, and a weakness, and I realized that I was running a fever. I took my temperature and saw that it was 102°, and I took him and went to my parents.

My husband had just traveled overseas in order to interview Julia Roberts, and I couldn't bear the thought of staying alone for another minute with this fragile little creature. I was terrified like I had never been before in my life. I loved him like I'd never loved anyone in my life. I was helpless like I had never been before in my life.

I lay in the bath, at my parents' house, for hours, because only in the hot water could I somehow tolerate the pain of my milk-bursting breasts. I was in so much pain that I couldn't even hold the baby in my arms. I phoned the doctor and hysterically asked him to help me stop this volcano raging within me. He told me to try to continue expressing milk; I told him that I'd been trying for hours, and that it was as painful as cutting into my raw flesh. He told me that there was a way to stop the milk, but it would stop it for good, and I wouldn't be able to resume breast-feeding. Considering the fact that I was burning up with a fever, that I was hurting like I'd never thought I could hurt, and that I was horrified by the thought that I had almost killed my son, the only creature that I had ever been responsible for, I found it odd to discover how difficult it was for me to stop breast-feeding. My mind was filled with all those studies conducted on breast-feeding, which are published every couple of days, about how children who are breast-fed longer are healthier, stronger, and smarter, and suddenly I realized how much power there is in being a breast feeding mother, and how much I loved it, how I loved the power of being a source of life and having no replacement.

Even though I was in pain, even though I was wearing silicon nipples, and even though my nipples were bruised, I was the one giving him something that no one else could. I was the only one who, until now, could provide for his needs – all his needs. No one else could do anything with my wailing infant but hand him over to me, the beatific mother. Only I had this immense power. Only I contained this divine product abundant with health-giving properties, and everything he needed for his intelligence and his future. And I was going to give it all up. I was going to take it away from him. I cried into the bathwater, and my tears mixed with the milk that leaked from my breasts.

The dear doctor told me to bind cabbage leaves onto my breasts, as tightly as I could, and after several hours, it would dry up all the milk. I told him that I wanted something less stupid than cabbage. We aren't living in the Middle Ages, and I wanted a pill. He said that there is a risk that anti-lactation medications cause cancer.

I went to the refrigerator, put cabbage leaves on my breasts, and tied an elastic bandage around myself. I had never looked as stupid as I did at that moment, with the cabbage peeking out of my décolletage. And then my man called. He had just finished interviewing Julia. "What's she like?" I asked. "Amazing," he replied, and then added that she was much thinner then he thought she'd be. I took a bite out of the cabbage leaves peeking from my plunging neckline, and while I nibbled on them, I told him that he didn't have to hurry back home. Now I felt seriously shitty. Not that I could take on Julia Roberts on a regular day, but this was definitely an unfair battle.

I desperately wanted to be a good mother, a mother who gave everything she had. Yes, I had also read that there was no such thing as a perfect mother, and a woman had to make do with being a good-enough mother, but I didn't want to be a good-enough mother. Just like I didn't want to be a good-enough photographer. I didn't want to be *good enough* at anything. I wanted to be a great mother, a charming, wonderful mother, and not just an *all-right* mother. That wasn't the reason I had conceived a child. That wasn't why I had left the professional path. That wasn't why I had lain in bed for six months. That wasn't why I had gained all these extra pounds. Not to be average. I had a baby because I wanted to be wonderful. To fly high on the wings of the purest and truest love of them all, the love of a mother for her child. I did it in order to realize my femininity, to be a wonderful mother from the fairy tales.

And the cabbage stopped my milk supply.

Completely.

> I usually don't write in, but this time I must.
> When I retired from a glamorous career in
> advertising in favor of raising my children, and
> a different job, which I do from home, I did it
> willingly, motivated by my internal need as a
> mother. We understand that you didn't breast-
> feed your children and occasionally you incite
> against breast-feeding and denigrate it, but
> isn't there a limit? Don't you think you've said
> enough?
>
> Ella

"How long did you breast-feed?" How many times did I hear
that question? During every visit to the pediatrician, at every
child development checkup, and mostly during discussions
with women. "It's a shame that you didn't breast-feed for a
more extended period," they told me so many times, so many
women. "It's so magical, and important, and wonderful. Nothing
is healthier than breast-feeding. You could have. After all, you
had milk; every woman has milk. It's the most natural thing in
the world." But it wasn't natural for me. It wasn't at all like in the
movies, with the pleasant background music, the entire house
white and gleaming, and with the smile of the happy and tranquil
mother that I was supposed to be. Instead my house looked like a
garbage dump, and I looked like a piece of junk that someone had
forgotten there, and that's how I felt, and it was so painful, and I
never knew if he was full or not, and "I couldn't," I answered.

*And I didn't want to,* but I didn't say that, because you don't
say that you didn't want to, but that you couldn't, and hope that

someone, preferably a woman, will say that it's okay that you couldn't. But no one said that it was okay. All those women, who breast-fed for a year or two years, always told me that it was a matter of willpower, and that it's a shame, because I have no idea what I missed, and there were those who went as far as insisting on telling me what I had snatched away from him and accompanied those admonishing words with that condescending expression that only those who have seen the light can muster. So I'd tell them that he choked. "It happens," said the enlightened ones. "It's a shame that you didn't see a lactation consultant." A shame. "Yes, it really is a shame," I'd answer and lower my eyes, going back to that first time in my life when I held a human creature who wasn't breathing – the first and sole creature in the world for whom I was responsible. And I felt terrible guilt. I felt like such a failure.

And he wasn't even two months old. And until then I had been so successful.

> I'm a student and it annoys me that so many people who have never set foot on the campus, and certainly not in the Faculty of Exact Sciences, think it is their right to tell me all the time that I'm at such a wonderful period of my life. Next time you write about something that you have no idea about, try to survive one semester, or one week, in our shoes, and deal with an endless stream of assignments/tests/exams, and when you have some free time you study a bit more and when you have another spare second you have to prepare an essay and in between, you're trying to catch up on your sleep. The most wonderful period of my life?! I hope not.
>
> Danya

# 6

*And [she] took the child, and laid it in her bosom,*
*and became nurse unto it.*

(Ruth 4:16)

After about two months, when the princess's body recoups, and she grows used to those odd sleeping hours, and getting up at night, and breast-feeding flows along peacefully, the princess starts enjoying motherhood. Now they're two, she and the tiny heir. Connected. She's his mother. No one else in the world knows him like she does; no one else knows what he needs like she does; no one else calms him down like she does. Taking care of him fills her with joy, and their magical moments increase by the minute, filling her with a feeling of genuine worth, of fulfillment. This little creature, with a pinch from her and a pinch from the prince, and the gaze that he fixes upon her, melts her. She wanders around with the stroller, after it took her an hour and a half to fold it, put it in the car, change his clothes because he spat up for the millionth time, and change his diaper.

And now, finally, she's at a café with a friend, and everyone passing by sticks their head into the stroller, to catch a glimpse of the miracle, and says what a lovely baby, so sweet, and her face glows, and her heart blossoms with happiness, and then he starts crying, and she pulls out her breast in the middle of the street as if it's the most natural and majestic thing in the world, and her single girlfriend thinks that it's the most wonderful thing, and marvels at how amazing she is, and how does she know that that's what he needs, and how does she do it, and the princess is in seventh heaven. She knows that she's touching the truth of life. She's a mother.

And just then, just when everything begins to flow peacefully, when she starts enjoying herself, and singing to him, and teaching him things, and he starts showing interest and smiling, and she buys him black-and-white pictures, and toys that will develop her Baby Mozart, the prince and the princess have to decide what to do next.

The princess's maternity leave is almost over. The heir will be three months old in no time at all. And the princess, even though she's exhausted, and she's hauling around an extra twenty pounds, knows that there's nothing more important than what she's doing: being a mother. It's a lot more important than any job or any vacation abroad, or anything else she ever did. *Everything else can wait*, she says to herself; she'll have enough time to live the rat race when he grows up a bit. She can't even think about leaving him now. Nothing is more important than her bond with him, this bond that will serve as the foundation for his self-confidence, that will serve as the foundation for his entire emotional world. So they sit down to talk about it. To decide.

She, in her rags, cradling her heir against her bosom, and across from her, the prince, who just came home from work and kicked off his shoes one minute ago, and they look at their baby, and he looks so tiny and helpless, and each of them thinks about all those psychological studies that state how important this period is in defining the rest of the heir's life. Especially his emotional life. Every mistake that they make now, they fear, may scratch his gentle soul and leave it bruised and bleeding forever. And they'll be to blame. Because it all begins at home.

> I know that my boys are still small, and everyone says that there's still so much time, but I just can't understand how I'm expected to raise them, and spoil and love them, and then, at the age of 18, they'll be whisked away to the army. I know that this is because we, as Jews, have no other country, but I'm a mother trying to protect my children and prevent traumas, and it's hard for me to deal with this. I feel that I have to do something. I just don't know what.
>
> Jordana

The prince and princess know that if the princess returns to work, they are left with two options: a nanny or a day care center. They look at the tiny heir and can't imagine him amongst other children, not receiving all the attention and the warmth and love he needs; they can't think of him crying without being held immediately in a pair of loving arms. They agree that he is definitely too small for day care. They are left with the nanny option. They calculate the cost of a nanny, and realize that whether it would be part-time or full-time, the nanny would earn almost as much as the princess while working similar hours. Now, they ask themselves, is it worth it for the little bit of money that would be left after paying the nanny that their heir – who until three months ago wasn't even here and is now the most important thing in their world, his welfare being paramount – should be forced to pass through a stranger's hands, and who knows what they'd inflict on him, what kind of scars and damages, and all this for a handful of pennies?

The princess, who has anyway taken a break from the rat race and is immersed in the pleasure of being a mother, can't think of parting with the heir for an entire day. Besides, she is still breast-feeding. If she leaves him for an entire day, she'll have to stop breast-feeding him. It seems like a terrible injustice to inflict upon him. True, she could express milk. That's what the prince and the princess say, and then they look at him again, at their tiny, fragile heir, and they know. They know that the best and the right thing to do now is to leave him with his mother a bit more. Nothing is more important than being with him, than giving him her love, than being close to him and him being close to her. He needs her so much right now, and she wants to be there for him. To give him the security, strength, warmth, and love that he so needs now, this perfect, wonderful creature. And she wants to stay with him and help him be wonderful and perfect. And he needs her for that, because she is the only one investing and loving and giving him everything he needs, in just the amount that he needs.

She looks at him and he is so small and so new and so hers that she can't think of leaving him now, of being away from him for so many hours, not knowing what might be happening to him at any given moment. That's not why she conceived him. Not so she could cast him away into a stranger's hands, and certainly not for the few pennies left over at the end of the month.

Hi. A friend gave me an idea a long time ago, while I was deliberating about the same topic: calculate the domestic income of both the husband and the wife. When you measure the cost of child care against your combined income instead of just against the mother's income, going out to work

seems more logical and worthwhile. At least for
your spirit.

P.S. My son will soon be going to a public
kindergarten, so we won't have to pay for the
private preschool anymore, and if I cut down
my job to part-time, it's more worthwhile than
signing him up for afternoon child care.

Or maybe I'll listen to my own advice…

Amelia

Eight months had passed since that afternoon in which the kind
doctor ordered me to get into bed and quietly expand. My son
was already almost three months old, and I could leave him for
a couple of hours with a babysitter or a grandmother, and after
so many months of lying at home, of suffocation, and later the
months of panic and life revolving around him, of changing
diapers, bathing, mumbling babyish endearments, breast-feeding
and then bottle feeding, of rocking, and walking around with a
stroller, I felt that I had to just get out for a minute. I wanted to
do something. Something else. Something that wasn't related to
caretaking.

Although I had already closed my studio, because I couldn't pay
rent for a place that stood empty, I knew I could still take pictures.
Working out of my house was considered less prestigious and
required lugging my equipment, but I felt lucky to have a job that
would let me go away for only two or three hours. I knew nothing
bad would happen to my son as a result of several hours without
me. Perhaps it would even be better for him, because I'd go out a
bit, breathe some fresh air, and return home a nicer person.

I had always been a freelancer and had worked for several
places, but the bulk of my work was taking pictures for one

newspaper. I liked being a freelancer. I was paid according to the amount of work I handed in, and I didn't mind the hard work. When I started phoning everyone in order to announce my return to work, I didn't expect to be greeted like the messiah, but I didn't expect the answers that I received. "Congratulations, how's motherhood? How is he? Oh, work…well, sorry, but we didn't have a choice, so we found someone to replace you, and we feel a bit uncomfortable with the situation, but why don't you call next week and we'll see." And after a week they told me, "Maybe next week."

I understood them, all those people who wouldn't wait: the advertising firms, the theater. But I had a harder time understanding my editors at the paper, with whom I'd worked for more than six years. So I was insulted and hurt, but I decided to persist, and phone, and set up meetings, because they had known me for so long, and they liked my work. So it would take a little time to work my way back into their rotation – so what? Everything would be okay. I'd make the effort and squeeze back in, bit by bit.

The process was painstakingly slow. After all the meetings, the phone calls, and the smiles, I managed to get from the paper one or two shots a week. It wasn't even a quarter of what I had done for them before. One month passed, and then two, and during that period, in which I was busy trying to learn to be a mother and to squeeze myself back into the job market, I started having second thoughts.

Anyway, I was already immersed in this world of diapers and getting up at night. And anyway, I was only working part-time and I earned pennies that barely covered the cost of a nanny who was even more part-time than myself, and I barely left the house, all the more so in the evenings, and I didn't take trips anywhere. The only thing I wore was rags because it was stupid to buy clothes before I regained my figure, and it's not as if my biological clock had actually stopped. If the children were born close together it would be easier later on, so it was foolish to postpone another pregnancy, because it had taken me so long with the first one, and because I had a sweet fantasy about two children who'd be friends. Being the practical girl that I was, and because I also thought that it would be right and sensible, I thought to myself that there was no point in waiting. I did want another child. It was just so logical.

You wrote about the endless struggle trying to acquire a figure that will comply with our times. It doesn't matter if you're before, after, or in the midst of childbearing; I feel as though it's never enough, that I have to do more. And there are those kind souls who are quick to "encourage" you and tell you, "You look so great – you've already lost most of the weight" (almost one year since I gave birth). Well, thank you, really, and pardon me that this is my third child and that I had a healthy pregnancy, and pardon me for choosing to breast-feed and continuing to eat a nutritious and healthy diet even several months after.

And there are those who insist on telling you, "Oh, you look tired." I ran into one of those at the synagogue during the recent holiday. "Thank you," I replied, "and I'm also grouchy." "Oh? Why?" she asked. "I just am," I answered, "no special reason." And I smiled impassively.

So I say okay, the holidays are behind us, we're facing a new year, a new beginning. I am asking everyone's forgiveness and am forgiving everyone. I'm trying to be calm, pleasant, positive, and loving. I woke up on Sunday morning and went for a walk with my baby daughter, full of joy and happiness, thankful for the good things that I have in life, my family, my daughters, my husband (he's actually okay), grateful for the shining sun, the grass still sparkling from yesterday's rain and dew, and my sweet little doll, smiling from her stroller at the neighbor, who stopped me with a big smile and said, "How's it going? Did you maybe put on a few pounds during the holidays?"

Yael

# 7

*A joyful mother of children. Praise ye the LORD.*
(Psalms 113:9)

The princess decides not to go back to work, and to extend her maternity leave and stay with the heir at home for another few months. Since she's a serious and accomplished woman, she decides that if her role now is to be a mother, she'll excel in it. She'll dive headfirst into this huge ocean with all her soul and with lots of love and joy. She's fascinated with motherhood. It fills her up and becomes her sole interest. She enjoys examining it, wallowing in it, touching the foundations and heavens of this experience she'd heard so much about. The experience of being a mother. *The* mother. She searches for enrichment classes for her tiny heir and runs between Gymboree and swimming, reads him stories, and walks around with a big smile because she knows that she's doing the most important thing in the world.

Nothing is as important as what she's doing. Not even what the prince is doing, even though he has a slightly ramshackle kingdom to run. And she doesn't budge from the heir. She feels she's the only one who can understand him and fulfill all his needs in a way that is supremely accurate and correct. She tries several times, just for a moment, at noon, to put him in his room, the room that she decorated so prettily. She tries to put him in his own bed, but he cries so much that she feels as though her heart is breaking from knowing that he's lying all alone in his room, scared and lonely. She knows how much he needs to feel her next to him. She read in all the books about childrearing that if he doesn't feel her close to him, he could suffer later on in life – maybe for his entire life – from the trauma and fear of abandonment, so she just lets it go. For now she's not moving him out of their room, out of their bed.

She doesn't even want to leave him for several hours in the evening, just to go out. But since she *is* a princess, she has obligations and occasionally has to accompany the prince to formal affairs. So she wears a sour expression, just so he can see how miserable this makes her, and goes out only after giving the babysitter incredibly detailed instructions. The first two times they go out, she finds herself seated next to men. She, who was always involved, and opinionated, and considered herself someone who filled an important role in the kingdom's management, discovers that all the political arguments and all the babble about work and money no longer interest her. She tries talking with these men, next to whom she's seated, about the momentous experiences of her present life with her child, about the lovely progress that he's making, and what a charming boy he is, and the carrot that he has just started eating, and about how this is the real thing – this is true happiness and fulfillment.

As she speaks, she sees how their eyes start glazing over, and at the first possible opportunity, they turn their backs on her and start a conversation with whoever is sitting on the other side. *They can't understand*, she says to herself, *and it's their loss.* She knows the truth. She knows that what she's doing is more important than CEOing some company, or climbing the ladder of success and influence that goes nowhere. She pities them. She pities them for all they are missing, for not being able to understand, not being able to relate to these depths of emotion and excitement.

After these initial experiences, the princess insists on sitting next to women whenever they go out, especially those who have already experienced motherhood. During her deeply engrossing discussions with them, she finds herself talking about the new feelings that are overwhelming her. She swaps experiences with them, examines their opinions, learns from them, and little by little begins to find things that she can teach them as well.

During one of these dinners, she suddenly bursts into raucous laughter. Everyone turns to stare at her, and her mortified prince asks that she share her joke with them. She's silent for a moment, and then tells them something, but not what originally made her laugh. She knows that it won't amuse the prince if she tells everyone what really happened to her – how, just that day, in the afternoon, she couldn't bear it anymore, and she peed behind the bushes in the park. So she just makes something up, and no one laughs.

> Do you really think that bringing children into this world and putting them in a day care, or whatever it is, until five p.m. and working full-time is a way of life? Is this how we're supposed to function as mothers? To spend two hours with our children before they go to bed? When will you understand that this isn't the right way? That the reason that the entire younger generation looks like it looks is because they don't have a parent figure to look up to at home, and they have nannies raising them?!

Look how we were raised. Most of us grew up
with a mother at home and we turned out to be
a fine generation. Instead of learning from it,
mothers today do just the opposite, and the
results aren't encouraging. I chose to be a proud
and happy homemaker to four little children. If
you want a career, don't bring children into this
world. Because giving birth to them just so that
someone else will take care of them isn't the
right thing to do. Children have to be given a
warm home with at least one parent who is there
for them.

I find it important to mention that I'm not a
homemaker our of financial privilege. My husband
is a hired worker with only an average salary,
and we still manage splendidly, because we know
how to manage our house. We don't live a life of
luxury or indulgence. Yet we have everything we
need, thank God. And we aren't Orthodox. We chose
this way of life out of ideology. Believe me,
there are better ways than sticking a child in
day care for so many hours. We can forego riches
and careers for the sake of our children. Because
family is what counts, not material things.

Elinor

When my child turned four months old and several days, when
I had just started getting along with him and with myself, and
discovering the joy and pleasure of our togetherness, and it seemed
as though I was starting to get the dimensions of my butt under
control, I found myself hanging angels in the bathroom. Since the
world of kitsch had never been my favorite domain, and angels

never were my favorite decoration, I flew to the nearest pharmacy to buy a pregnancy test and discovered that it wasn't by chance that I had been decorating the bathroom in ethereal themes.

I was so happy. I'd have another baby and get it over with. My life had come to a halt anyway, and my work was just trudging along as it was, so now I'd have two children, and that's it – I'd be done with it and be able to continue onwards.

A week passed, and then several more, and my son was passing developmental milestones, extending his arms so I'd pick him up, and then crawling. We reorganized the entire house, putting everything up high so nothing would endanger him. Now I had to keep him busy – not only feed him and rock him, but play with him and go for walks with him. And with every passing day, with every passing minute during which I had to keep him occupied, I began realizing and internalizing that raising a child wasn't exactly the "okay-we-reproduced-it's-behind-us-let's-move-on" sort of thing that I'd thought it would be. And I started realizing that I was barely managing with one, and that I wasn't even sure that I was doing it well enough. And I started feeling scared.

I was scared that I wouldn't manage with two, that I wouldn't have the necessary strength for it, that I'd rob him of the attention he deserved and needed, that I wouldn't have the required patience, that I wouldn't know how to divide myself between the two of them; and I became terribly frightened. But that didn't stop my belly from growing. It just got bigger and bigger, growing with my fears and with the realization that I was living a role that I still didn't understand, a life that I still didn't feel was mine, a job description that I didn't really know how to fill.

*Hey*, I wanted to scream, *I'm just a girl.* The same girl who just recently galloped around town on her scooter fancy-free, who took pictures in all sorts of dangerous places, who danced almost every night until dawn, who was destined for greatness, who wanted to conquer the world. And there I was, in the public park, running, with my enormous belly, after my son, who was crawling through the filthy sand, realizing that soon enough I'd be a mother of two. I couldn't believe that this was happening to me, and I couldn't imagine how I'd manage. Even my weight gain came to a halt. During my first pregnancy, I had gained fifty pounds. During my second, I gained only twenty-five. Because who had time to eat?

You wrote, sadly, about the shorts that you decided you'd no longer wear. I thought so as well. And it became intolerable. I developed ugly lines of bitterness, an awful despair, and such an obsession toward my body and the mirror that I craved for old age to redeem me from my fixation on my inconsolable, unsatisfied, starved, and treacherous body. As a former photographer, you know how destructive it is to let an external glance – male, female, or your own – destroy your body image.

I come from this awful, painful, desperate misery, and I have no husband or children to comfort me because I wasted my twenties on my body image, on the worship of beauty, and on the things women put themselves through – diets and eating disorders and everything that causes me to cringe when I look back at those years. What a shame. You at least have a home, and a job, and all sorts of gifts, and a lot of luck. You have a place to contain your pain, and that's much

```
more important than shorts that will contain your
thighs. Don't be sad.
     Sarah
```

I was terrified of what the future held in store, and I felt more and more lost.

One day, one of my friends – who was single like all my friends at the time – called me. She talked enthusiastically about her new date and began a detailed report about what he said, what she said, and how he reacted, and how she giggled, and how he laughed, and what he did later on. When she stopped for a minute, I asked her if she ever felt like she doesn't have any time for herself.

She said that maybe I wasn't managing my time correctly; I should be more organized.

And I told her that wasn't what I meant. I meant that *feeling*. Did she ever feel that way also, as though she didn't have any air, that she was constantly giving and giving, and that she didn't have any more energy to run around; that she was fading away and nobody saw it, and nobody really appreciated her? Because that's how I felt – that I couldn't breathe.

And she was silent for a minute, and then said no. She had never felt that way.

I had never felt that way either, in my previous life. So out of control that I couldn't even shout, "Time out!" *Stop for a minute. I'll be back tomorrow. Just for today, let me put a blanket over my head and disappear. Only for one day. One day just to sleep. One day not to be. Not to take care of someone. Not to worry about someone. Not to be responsible. Not to look at the clock. To be with myself for just one moment.*

And she asked me if I thought she should call.

"Who?" I asked.

"The guy from yesterday."

"I don't know," I said.

And I felt so alone.

■ ■ ■

The prince loves the heir with all his heart. He's willing to sacrifice his life for him. When he returns from work in the evening, after eating, showering, and changing into casual clothes, he takes the heir from the princess's arms, holds him, and makes funny faces at him. He enjoys the heir's sweet smiles and the way he looks at him, and joy fills his heart. Then he lifts him up high, spins him around, and tosses him up in the air, even though it alarms the princess terribly and she shouts at him to be careful. He's impressed by the heir's bravery, how he isn't frightened, and he only smiles. Yes, that's his wonderful and brave heir. And then, after some time, the heir starts crying, because he's hungry.

The prince returns him to the princess, and watches with wonderment how she nurses him, and how gentle she is with him, and how she understands him, and knows him, and he is so overjoyed by this magnificent bond between her and the baby. Knowing that the princess is a good mother generates within him a feeling of confidence – a feeling that he chose right. And he just loves her more because of it. And he appreciates her. It's true that the bond between the princess and the heir has shoved him aside, but he knew that this would happen. He was prepared for it; he knew that it was a natural and right move and considers it a small price to pay compared to the enormous gain from the knowledge that the heir is in such good, loving hands.

The months pass, and the prince, who has to confront daily difficulties outside of the palace, at his work, fighting for their livelihood in the harsh world, wants to go on a vacation. He wants several days of peace and quiet with the princess, just the two of them. Maybe they'll manage to talk quietly, because it's been impossible to complete more than two sentences for some time now, and he wants to pamper her some; maybe she'll even order a massage, and rest. He wants her to sleep peacefully for just one night, without getting up for the heir, because he sees the black circles under her eyes, and maybe if she'll rest a bit, then she won't say "not tonight" because she's really tired, and they haven't done it in ages. But it isn't only that. He misses her. He misses their togetherness.

So one evening he suggests that they go on a short romantic vacation.

And she stares at him. She can't believe he's offering something like this. She's in shock. How can she, she tells him furiously: she's still breast-feeding! She can't leave the heir now! He can't even sleep without feeling her close to him. And he needs her so badly at this stage and she doesn't understand how he even thought of it. How could he have conceived this crazy, illogical, detached idea?

And the prince knows she's right, and that he hadn't really thought it through.

And he asks for her forgiveness.

# 8

*Thou that dwellest in the gardens,*
*the companions hearken to thy voice...*

(Song of Songs 8:13)

My man felt me fading away, and he arranged a vacation for us. A romantic vacation – just the two of us. I was happy to get away, and happy for the chance to be with him. So we went. And I didn't leave the room. I slept. And slept. And my man took joy in me and I in him. And we were both delighted by the quiet. By being together. And then I called to ask how the baby was faring. Apparently, he was running a bit of a fever and I heard him crying in the background. I couldn't breathe. I couldn't stand it any longer, and I wanted to go home, I wanted to go back, and my heart was torn, and I knew that until I held him, until I hugged him, until I was with him, I wouldn't be able to relax. I realized that the time hadn't come yet. That I couldn't go away yet. That I couldn't break away. And we went back.

And I returned to him, to our walks with the stroller.

One day, when I arrived at the park, to collapse on one of the benches, one hand rocking the stroller and the other one placed under the humongous breasts that were mine, but not really mine, and on my belly, the belly that for the past two years had become the window sill from which I gazed at the world, I heard fragments of conversation between the other mothers who shepherded their young ones within the restricted spaces of the fenced sandbox, the concrete paths and the minute patches of grass planted like oases in the middle of the asphalt expanses teeming with buses.

"Sweetie, don't touch the cat," said one mother. "Cola is bad," said another. "And so are antibiotics, and there's this excellent new stroller, and a wonderful ointment for diaper rash, and go take a pee, I'll keep an eye on him, and take a wipe with you." And one mother yelled at her friend, "What are you talking about? After the carrot you mash a sweet potato; that's the best thing to do." "And when do you start with the chicken?" asked someone else. I didn't know either when it was finally allowed to feed chicken to a baby. I edged closer. The next day I approached them and said hello, and they immediately responded cheerfully, and asked where I lived, and how old my baby was, and how many weeks pregnant I was, and by the next day, I was already one of them. I left the house with a purpose. No more wandering. No more walking around the city lonely and abandoned. I went to meet the group. The group of mothers in the park.

> It just kills me that sometimes I'm just dying to go out or sit with a friend and I don't. There are days when I simply cry with the pain. It may sound stupid to you (it sometimes sounds stupid to me), but I'm sick of eating my heart out and feeling lonely and stuck at home all the time with only myself as company.
> Gabriella

Within this group, I could release all the contradictory feelings that bubbled and burned within me. Here, I could go into the most precise details, and I was allowed to say that things were difficult for me. And from then on, every day when I didn't work, I went to meet them in the mornings. And on days that I managed to get some work for a few pathetic hours, I ran to them during the afternoons. To our fenced territory. The territory in which everyone was like me: overweight, with dark circles under their eyes, wearing only comfortable clothes. The only place in which I was right, and I felt right.

At that place, sandwiched between one busy street and another, hidden from the eye, I found consolation. And I found another thing. I discovered that I was part of something that I hadn't even known I yearned for, that I didn't even think I was interested in, that I was sure had disappeared from the world with equality and ambition: the world of feminine wisdom. A world with a magnificent past that was just waiting there. Waiting for a day when I'd need it, and now that I needed it, it extended its arms to me so that I'd come and snuggle up within it, find consolation and warmth in its loving and understanding embrace. In their embrace. I was allowed to feel things that up until then, I was sure I was forbidden to feel. And I could talk about it. And complain. Complain and they would understand me; complain and receive a big hug; complain and discover that everyone felt the same way, and that it's okay.

I joined the Public Park Union for Complaints, and it was a great pleasure. And mostly, we complained about them. About the men. About how they didn't understand, how they didn't share our entire world with us. How they didn't help like we expected them to, and didn't understand us, and didn't understand what they were missing. And so, we sat in a circle, just like generation after generation before us sat at the tent's entrance, throwing wood into the fire, guarding it so it would continue burning. And we sat within the boundaries of our territory, throwing our pain and frustration into the sandbox that reeked of cat urine, discussing and harping on our problems, our difficulties, and first and foremost, our complaints toward our men. These complaints burned brighter than the rest. The more we complained, the stronger was the fire. As it grew higher and higher and we became addicted to it, I was mesmerized. Inebriated.

I had a place. I was part of a group that was the continuation of a historical chain whose roots were planted way back in the beginning of time, its knowledge passed down from generation to generation, providing an anchor and the support of wisdom and comprehension for many generations of women. I was part of that same chain that my grandmothers before me had been part of, and their grandmothers before them, while they sat together in their kitchens, in the menstruation tent, near the stream while doing their laundry, pouring their hearts out, giving each other their wisdom and experience, empowering each other, sharing advice. And I no longer felt alone. I had wise guides who were glad to explain to me, teach me, and help me pave the way to real life. To building a family.

And I was happy to learn from them, especially from those who had clearly been running their own lives from the age of twelve, as well as the lives of those around them. And they'd been doing it with an iron fist, and they knew all the paths, the straight as well as the winding, to get what they wanted; they knew how to manipulate, and how to organize their lives like they wanted them to be. They knew the secret and they were willing to share it with me, and I swallowed every detail that they fed me. They had answers to all my questions. They knew what my baby had to eat, and when, and they knew the best doctor in the neighborhood, and the occupational therapy expert; they knew what to do for swollen legs and stretch marks, what to say to a husband and how to give an ultimatum.

Because for every dilemma that someone flung out into space, someone else always had advice. From her own personal experience. And after a time, I felt as though I understood more, and that I also had something to give and teach and bestow. I discovered that after peeling away the scooter and the cameras, I could touch something that I hadn't realized I had within me, that had been in hiding all my life and was suddenly exposed. I was part of a group that taught me something that I had never known before. They taught me how to be a woman.

I heard so much brilliant advice. I gave so much valuable advice back. *Tell him, notify him, resign, keep quiet, yell, put your foot down, let me give you a tip about blow jobs, I know what kind of exercise you really, really need, you must go to my doctor, he's the best, and buy my bra, it's the most comfortable, and never, under any circumstances, let your kids eat in front of the television, I don't allow mine, you're making a mistake, you're too weak, you're too tough, why didn't you ask me, it's such a shame that you didn't ask me, if only you'd asked me, I would have organized your entire life.*

I loved them, my supportive circle of women from the park. I worshipped them. I didn't really care about their credentials. It didn't matter to me that I received advice on relationships from someone who had just gotten a divorce, advice on work from someone who didn't work, advice on preschools from someone who didn't send her children to preschool, advice on diets from someone who weighed more than myself. And I listened to them. I became a different person thanks to the training that I received in the park. I learned how to manipulate, how to say only half of what I wanted to say, how to maintain a sour silence, how to say something poisonous under the guise of amicability. I was mastering the art of being a woman. I even grew my hair.

I didn't care that their asses didn't look like Jennifer Lopez's, that they didn't know my man. Now that I knew how to be a woman, and what I had to do, I was set on my goal, and I had a plan. Now I was clear on how I wanted to live, how I wanted my family to be and to function. Equipped with support, advice, and information that I gathered around the sandbox, I believed that if I tried hard enough, in a short while, toward the birth of my baby girl, I'd make my life look like a perfect picture. I was prepared and ready to charge toward my goal. I had all the required material. I had a father, a mother, a little boy, and soon I would add a baby girl. Now, all I had to do was place everyone exactly how I dreamed I'd position them, and they'd look just like I dreamed they would, smile at the camera, and say cheese.

Every time my mother comes to visit, everything that's obvious and that usually weighs down on me comes out in the open in the most dramatic and grave manner. "The back of the baby's head is flat. It's so alarming" (he's four months old and ever since he turned two weeks old I've been running with him to physiotherapy); "Oh, God, look at those mosquito bites that your child has on her" (I just installed a hundred-dollar screen door); "Allow me to just say that you have to make the effort to dress up and look pretty for your husband inside your house" (I don't want to! I'll go around with my hair in a ponytail because every time I pick up the baby he tears my hair out. And I'll wear my pajamas because it's more comfortable this way. Anyway, my husband thinks that I'm pretty just as I am, and if Billy Bob Thornton cheated on Angelina Jolie, then it doesn't really leave much hope for us lesser mortals).

This week she just went on and on and I listened and justified myself, until finally, I felt that if I didn't shut her up, I'd go out of my mind. And I told her (or in all honesty, I screamed at her) that I've had enough, and if I'm not asking for her opinion, that I don't need her to give it to me voluntarily, and that she has to stop making me feel as though I'm inadequate like only she knows how to. When I was done, she stormed out of the house and slammed the door behind her.

I just stood there. I felt like an awful person who speaks atrociously to her mother who went through all the trouble of raising her (which is probably why my daughter will someday talk to me in the exact same way; it will be my punishment), and maybe I'm actually crazy and I'm in urgent need of hospitalization. Then, I read what you wrote and you reassured me that I'm only normal. Today, I'm going to introduce my mother to you.

Talia

# 9

*She findeth no rest...*

(Lamentations 1:3)

Before the baby was born, I started searching for a good preschool for my son. I checked and examined the technique of wiping runny noses in half a million places that were recommended to me by the park women, and I found the most wonderful place in the world. It also cost more than the others, which proved to me its excellent quality. For a two-month acclimatization period, I came with my son once every two days for one hour, then one hour with me and two without, then every day for half a day. And when he could finally stay there all by himself, and leave me one wonderful solitary moment for myself, the preschool teacher announced that she had received a fantastic offer to manage a boutique and in one week she was closing the preschool. She was very excited about her new challenge. She wasn't very interested in the fact that the week she was closing was the exact week I was due to give birth. Thoroughly frightened, I started searching for another place and shoved my child into the first one I found that was willing to accept him.

And then, my man received a job offer that he simply couldn't refuse. A promotion that would greatly improve our financial situation, but included crazy working hours. He was worried about me because he was a wonderful and involved husband, and he saw that I wasn't at the height of my glamour. We sat together and decided that this was a once-in-a-lifetime offer and he had to give it a go. Give it a few months. And I encouraged him because I wanted to be what I had promised him to be: his friend, his partner. So I told him that everything would be all right, that he didn't have to worry because I was strong and I could manage, and I had gone through harder things and we had promised to help each other achieve our dreams, ride wildly on that roller coaster called life, and not be afraid. I was determined to be a wonderful wife and he was terribly busy, so I'd make more of an effort. It was a fantastic offer, and it would help all of us, the entire family. It was for the family.

I gave birth. I was the mother of a newborn baby girl and a thirteen-month-old boy. And I thought that if only I tried hard enough, I'd succeed. Because I'd been told, my entire life, that it depended only on me.

▪ ▪ ▪

The princess knows it's time to send the heir to preschool. He's already two years old. Two years during which she has been with him almost every minute. Only recently she has managed to teach him to fall asleep without nursing, but he still can't fall asleep without her stroking him, without her singing him his regular songs, and every time she goes out in the evening, rare as that is, her departure is accompanied by his heart-wrenching sobs. She knows how sensitive he is, how much he needs her, but she also knows that he already needs the company of other children. So she signs him up for preschool. After the first days, during which both of them cry terribly, they adjust, she and the heir, to the separation. It's a relatively short separation, because the program is over by one o'clock and she doesn't sign him up for afternoon care. She decides that half a day is enough for him because he needs the quiet, he needs his home, and a full day away is still too much for him. And for her. Maybe next year she'll leave him until four.

Now the princess has several free hours during the morning. She starts taking care of things that have been neglected for so long. Especially the palace. She invests all her energy in it, all her free time. She wants to resume her hostess duties, and she, who can't go to sleep if there's a dirty cup in the sink, certainly can't entertain guests if the palace isn't shining. Little by little, the princess restores the palace's former shiny façade. She organizes, polishes, and embarks on a series of small renovations and paint jobs. When she entertains guests, she does everything alone. She cooks, bakes, and decorates the room with candles because it's important to her that everything be perfect.

She also signs up for exercise classes. She compares prices of gym subscriptions, just as she shops around with everything that she buys, because she's trying to save money. She's modest, even though she's a princess, because that's how she was raised, to content herself with little. To give and not to take. To do the best she can. To be gentle. Not to push. She's not like that. She's not like those women who'll do anything to get what they want, who are inconsiderate of others. No. She's a good woman. Whenever she's needed, she's there for everyone. For the heir, for the prince, for her friends. She never puts herself on top of her list of priorities. First and foremost, she thinks about the welfare of others. And she doesn't just waste money. For herself, she buys only the essentials. She's the type who doesn't need a lot. On the other hand, she pampers others gladly. She'll buy a friend a present that she'd never buy for herself. She cooks her son his favorite food and cooks the prince his favorite food. She eats the leftovers, and it doesn't bother her one bit.

She knows that the kingdom's financial situation isn't very good now, and the mortgage on the palace is burdensome, and the preschool tuition is heavy, but it really is an excellent place, and she's not willing to compromise on that. Anyway, the prince agreed with her that it's extremely important that the preschool be excellent, private, and small, so she's doing everything she can to scrimp and save. She asks her friends about sales, she paints the children's room all by herself, she travels out of town to search for bargains, and she manages to redecorate the palace with pennies.

At the end of the month, when the prince goes over their bills, his expression conveys to her that he's worried about all the expenses, and sometimes he asks if a certain something was necessary, and she's terribly insulted. He doesn't understand just how much she's been economizing; he doesn't understand what an effort she puts into saving, and how little she buys for herself.

Only very rarely, when she's in a really bad mood, does she suddenly find herself splurging on a pair of shoes, because she can't help herself, because all her friends have such beautiful clothes and shoes and she wants some as well. And anyway, she deserves it. She, who gives everyone everything, who relinquished all her dreams in order to be a good mother, and a good woman, and all she does all day is make sure that everyone has everything, and that the palace is polished, she also deserves some pampering once in a while. And she doesn't say anything to the prince about the shoes. When they go out, she wears them and he doesn't even notice, and she's glad that he doesn't notice. She doesn't feel like giving him a report about why she bought them and how much she paid. She starts thinking about going back to work, but they want more kids, so there's really no point in waiting anymore. And the princess doesn't renew her gym subscription because they're pregnant again.

> From the early hours of the morning, I wait for noon to roll around so that they'll go to sleep, and when they wake up, I am already planning ahead for the evening bath. I bathe them at 7:45 in the evening, there's a story immediately after that, and then straight to bed. I need this time for myself, this quiet. My husband calls me a robot.
>
> Every morning I say, "Grow up, already; get married and leave home," and they're still tiny (two and a half years old and eight months). Everyone keeps telling me to enjoy it while they're still small, because it just gets harder as they grow up. But for now, it's hard enough for me to get up at six o'clock in the morning to the sounds of the baby crying, and his brother harassing me and calling out, "Mommy, he's crying!"
>
> Kayla

When my baby girl was two months old, I took her to the doctor to weigh her, check her reflexes, and measure her head. "Everything's just fine," said the wonderful doctor, and then, without any preliminary warning, I collapsed into the chair and burst into tears, and through those tears I mumbled that I'm not managing. She ordered me to get a sitter today and go have a coffee by myself. On the way back home, I stopped by my son's preschool and peeked through a hole in the gate. A neighbor who was passing by saw me peeking and tutted while casting a pitying glance at my baby napping in her stroller. Shaking her head decisively, the neighbor expressed her firm opinion that I shouldn't sign the baby up for this preschool.

"Why?" I asked.

"You don't know how much they cry," she said. "Sometimes it tears my heart out and I think that they're simply left to fend for themselves." And even though I knew it wasn't true, and even though I had already cried plenty that day, I cried again. At that moment I decided to move my son to a big, established place. I wanted a staff; I wanted an inspector who would observe everything. I no longer wanted a small, personal, special, intimate place. I wanted somewhere secure. I went to a big day care center and settled down in their office until they signed him up for the next year. And I also signed up my new baby. I would have to wait six months for that moment to come. At the time, it seemed as though that day would never arrive. The mere thought that one day I'd get up in the morning and leave both of them somewhere for several hours, without having to take care of them, worry about them, run after them, and feel like a terrible mother, seemed to me like a sweet fantasy that was entirely out of reach. Through this veil of exhaustion and guilt, going to work suddenly seemed to me like a vacation. And I was desperate to return to work.

Last year I gave birth to a lovely baby girl (my second). I stayed at home with her for five months. Bit by bit, I felt depression overwhelming me. I felt that if I didn't leave the house with makeup and without someone hanging around my neck, I'd collapse. I envied my husband for having the privilege of going to work, meeting people, and having a genuine, civilized conversation that wasn't about "what she did today." I had thought that it would improve with the second child, and that you no longer have this itch to get out of the house and go to work, but I realized that staying at home wasn't for me.

Ilana

Experience had taught me how hard it is to work your way back into the job market. As I knew how problematic it is to disappear from the eyes of your employers for too long, after my baby girl was born, well before my three months of maternity leave were over, I started calling the newspaper I worked for. Even though this time I had been away for a much shorter period (since this time I had not been on bed rest and had worked throughout the pregnancy), I once again discovered that many things could change in such a short time. Once again, some of the editors had been replaced; new photographers had arrived on scene and were the rising stars of the moment. They were young, and willing to do anything, at every hour and at half the price, just to get themselves started. Again I found myself fighting. I, who just two years ago had been swamped with work and could pick and choose the jobs I wanted, who had a dusty catalog lying at home of my one-woman exhibition, who thought I had reached the promised land, found myself scrabbling for some crumbs like a new photographer. After several weeks, I managed to get one or two assignments a week from the newspaper.

A few months passed and I wasn't getting more assignments. In fact, I was getting fewer. But I insisted on being on constant standby, waiting for them to call. I tried putting together several hours of sleep, between his teething and her waking up to eat every few hours. I made sure I had a standby babysitter whom I could alert when the moment arrived and I was urgently summoned, and I didn't miss even one phone call, because maybe that would be the call that would send me to work. My salary was per photo. During those months, I earned less than half of what I paid my babysitter to be on call for me.

Already after the first baby I had had no success returning to work for the advertising agency and the rest of the places I had done occasional work with before, because they really didn't have any obligation to me. But the newspaper had been my home. I'd worked there for eight years. I didn't want to throw away everything I had achieved and give up on everything I had built, even if all that was left of my successful career was some pathetic leftovers. I decided to grit my teeth and continue trying to juggle all the balls in the air, all the while hoping that they wouldn't fall and shatter. *Two little babies and one part-time job,* I cheered myself on: that was the whole story. I reminded myself that I had already taken pictures in warzones, I had been beaten up in demonstrations, and I would manage.

Then, that phone call came through. On the other side of the line, the producer, a twenty-something-year-old, laid it out for me. The editor wanted me to travel two and a half hours that afternoon to Be'er Sheva – in the south of Israel – to take pictures of a family.

"But today's Friday," I said.

A silence descended on the line. We both recalled our last two conversations. After almost three weeks during which I hadn't received any work, I had phoned to ask what was going on, and if

I could speak to the editor. He had told me that she was busy and that he'd leave her a message. Two days later, when I still hadn't gotten any response and I'd been sitting by the phone like a junkie, I called again. Once again, she couldn't talk to me but she had left him instructions on what to say to me. He tried to avoid saying it. I asked him to tell me. He tried to weasel out of it again. I told him that I knew it wasn't coming from him, and he should just say it already, because my dignity could only go so low. So he said that she said that either I go out on any assignment I'm given, or I won't work there anymore. Because she won't work with prima donnas.

And I knew that my dignity had just reached rock bottom.

And I didn't go to Be'er Sheva that Friday afternoon.

And no one called me from the place where I had worked for eight years to say goodbye. They still haven't.

> We are the same age. Give or take two years. I'm sitting and writing even though it's late, and the children are sticking close to me in the living room (my husband is doing army reserve duty), because it's now or never. We have two little children. I would have another ten (it all depends, of course, on our financial situation), because apart from the fun of a big family gathering around the table, in childrearing I'm the one with the authority.
>
> All our lives we have to meet the standards that society and our parents outlined for us. We have to finish high school, go to the army, study in university, get married, have kids, and find a good job. I passed through all of the above with relative success – even my mother approved – until I got to the work part. I am 32 years old

and I can't make up my mind about what I want to do when I grow up. All the things I want to do are considered impractical, and I am, after all, a practical and conventional girl. Furthermore, my situation is pretty golden right now (not exactly 24-karat, but it's shiny nonetheless), and who wants to give up a good thing?

Anyway, my second, wonderful child came along (a shame that you can't give birth to the second one first) and here I am, at home for an entire year, having the time of my life, and what's more important is that I don't have to prove anything to anyone. People ask me what I do and I say, "Me, well, I'm at home with my son." "Oh, that's great, good for you." And that's that. No competition, no colleagues, no annoying bosses, no getting stuck hysterically in traffic at four in the afternoon. The house is always clean, there's food in the fridge, there's no guilty conscience. And everyone's happy – and that, miracle of miracles, includes my husband.

When I told my mother that on the day I decide that I've had enough of being home with the kids I'll be really sad, because then I'll no longer be doing the one job that is uniquely mine, without competition from others, she laughed and said, "Stop talking nonsense." What she meant, of course, was *wait till your children reach their teens*.

My husband says that it's my decision to make, and on this point I'm glad that I'm not a feminist, because the burden of bringing a salary home falls on him and it suits me just fine.

That's it. I did it. I'll send this letter quickly without rereading it because after a proofreading, all my inner truths will be erased and only the clichés will remain.

Miriam

# 10

*Give me, I pray thee, a little water of thy pitcher to drink...*

(Genesis 24:43)

In the evening, after my shower, I approached the mirror. Only three years had passed since that young woman with short hair and fire in her eyes had looked back at me. I let go of the towel in order to put cream on my bruised and bleeding nipples, and looked at my breasts lying there like deflated helium balloons forgotten under the sofa, at my stomach with its flabby rolls leaning on each other, at the lank hair that hadn't seen a hairdresser for months. And then there was my brain, which hadn't read a book for more than a year and a half. Now the thirty-year-old woman who was me looked back at me from the mirror with those same eyes, but there wasn't any excitement in them. Just an endless ocean of exhaustion and lethargy.

After weeks in which I had wandered the streets or sat in public parks rocking the twin stroller, which contained my son and my baby girl, regardless of the heat or the cold or the dark, trying to find a moment in which neither of them needed me to feed them, diaper them, give them something to drink, clean, soothe, burp, pick up, all I wanted was to go to my parents on Friday, eat something, and have someone hold and hug *me* for a change – have someone, for one minute, take care of me.

But my editor wouldn't work with a prima donna.

And I knew she was right. I couldn't deliver the goods. She wasn't running a charity organization. She was running a business, and she wanted to employ people who would be available at every given moment, who could jump to her every alert, who were grateful for every call. Yet I was still angry. I was angry that I had been fired. I was angry that I wasn't earning money. I was angry about how I looked. And what made me the angriest was that I felt as though I had been cheated. I was angry for having been told that it was all up to me, that nowadays, raising kids and working isn't a problem, which caused me to believe that times have changed, that there is no difference between men and women, that you can do everything if you just want it enough. And I wanted, I desperately wanted, and I made the effort, and I worked my ass off, but I didn't make it.

And I still didn't know that things were going to get much worse.

> This time you led me to the sofa in my parents'
> living room. I'm trying to take a nap and they're
> asking the grandchildren to be quiet because
> Mommy's sleeping. I told my husband that I'm
> also a little girl, who sometimes needs to be
> taken care of. You're writing about yourself,
> and actually, you're writing about me, and I'm
> crying. We could've been friends.
> Ora

The prince and the princess have an heiress, a little sister to the heir. At night, the princess gets up to nurse the heiress, and in the morning, she tries to take advantage of the hours during which the heir is in preschool to do some shopping and tidy the palace; and there are so many errands to run. In the afternoon she takes the heir to his afternoon activities with the baby, and then they return home for dinner, bath, and bedtime. She no longer reads the heir two stories at bedtime. She barely has the energy for one.

And around the time that she's utterly exhausted, the prince comes home. He arrives at home after dealing, all day long, with dragons that threatened him, that endangered his status, his promotion, that tried to overtake him and leave him far behind; and he's been fighting them. He fights with all his might, trying to prove himself, staying one more hour, two more hours, trying to be the best, to receive a raise. And he doesn't do this for himself; he's doing it for his family. For his princess and heirs, for the mortgage on the palace, for their future, so he can give them everything they need. And when he arrives home, to the princess for whom he fought, for whom he built the palace, he desperately wants to tell her about his victories and wants her to be proud of him. And there are bad days too, days when he fails, days when it seems as though nothing is working. Then, the only thing he wants is to come home already, meet his princess, lay his head in her embrace, and hear a kind word of solace from her, from his friend. From his love.

When he opens the door, he discovers a depleted princess.

The princess doesn't have the patience to hug or express appreciation. She wants him to be the one who's impressed, who appreciates, and she can't understand why he doesn't make the effort to come home earlier, why he doesn't think about her sometimes. Why he doesn't think about how difficult things are for her, and why he doesn't try to come home before darkness descends. One day, when she tells him that the heir has his end-of-the-year school party, he says that he doesn't know if he'll be able to make it, and she gets terribly upset. *He doesn't know how to distinguish between what's important and what isn't,* she says to herself. *His priorities always were confused.* Yes, she knew that before. Back when she fell in love with him she knew that she'd have to teach him a thing or two, but she thought it would be a piece of cake. She believed that after the wedding, she'd be able to do it without any problem. She'd teach him. But he didn't learn.

He isn't sensitive enough. He doesn't court her sufficiently or doesn't court when and how she prefers. He works too much but he isn't getting the promotions that she expected him to, or supporting her like she expected him to. He doesn't function like the caring and sharing father he promised to be, and he doesn't cook, or he does but leaves the kitchen filthy. And he's too tough with the heir, or too soft with him, and he barely spends time with the heiress. And he doesn't talk to her about his feelings, and he's not exactly interested in hers, or he is but not genuinely, or he loses patience in the middle, and she doesn't understand why he insists on putting his heart and soul into work, and why he doesn't try to spend more time with them. With her and the children.

In the end, he comes to the end-of-the-year party but she sees that he isn't as excited as she expected him to be and she's terribly disappointed with him. And he doesn't tell her what a mess he left behind at work and that he got into a lot of trouble because he insisted, on that particular day, on leaving early.

```
The day that my own personal serenity arrives
will be the day that I'll stop the devil's dance,
the exhaustion, and the race for survival. It
```

will be a kind of day when I'll wake up in the morning and my body won't ache because I'll allow someone to take care of me. It will be a day when I'll walk into the neighborhood supermarket and for once I'll be able to buy whatever I feel like buying. Yes, it will also be the day when I'll collect all the bills hanging on the refrigerator door and pay them, all at once.

On this day, I'll go out with my daughter for a morning of fun (cafes, shopping sprees in the mall), and fantasize about a weekend in a rural bed-and-breakfast with a good friend. I may even go as far as daring to order a plane ticket to some magical destination in one of the neighboring islands in the Middle East (because New Zealand shall remain a fantasy).

And I'd also like to decide that on this day, I'll resign from all my extra part-time jobs and focus only on one. Decide something and do it! On this day, I'll get a house cleaner, even if it's just a one-time thing. And what I'd like most of all, on the day that serenity comes, is to give more to those who don't even dare to dream of the day when serenity comes.

A single mother

My baby girl wasn't easy. *That's just how some kids are*, I said to myself. That's what everyone said to me. She still woke up many times every night. I got up with her, and the days and nights turned into an inseparable jumble of getting up and lying down. During the morning, I was with her, and in the afternoon, I was with both of them, trying to scrape the remains of my patience from the bottom of my barrel of resources. When she turned nine months old, when I no longer remembered how to sleep a full night, or what a pub looks like inside, when I no longer had any idea who I was or what I had ever wanted in life, the day arrived when I left her at the day care center and went to have a coffee. Alone. Without rocking the stroller, sticking a pacifier in anyone's mouth, pulling out a breast, mixing milk, changing diapers. An hour went by. And then another. I watched all the people walking down the street, those in a hurry and those not. Those who have time. And suddenly I felt odd having nothing to do. With my hands. With myself.

The next day, I told my man that I wanted to go away for one day. That I wanted to celebrate. Go to a hotel, sleep, pamper myself. Spend twenty-four hours in complete silence. The next day, I brought the children to day care and went to the train station. I could have driven, but I chose to travel by train. Maybe so I could feel far away. I sat on the train, and during the hour-long train ride, I filled the notepad that I had bought at the station. When the ride ended, I had chapter headings for a novel. A novel about four women, together in a room, who have all just given birth. I still had to write it, this novel, but I had a beginning. And I had the foundation. And from the moment I arrived at the hotel, all I did was sleep. I slept peacefully, as I hadn't slept for what seemed to me like forever.

> Many times, I just want to stop everything, and everyone can go to hell for all I care. And I'll just do whatever I want to do. These moments in which we shake off responsibilities toward the various people in our lives and do something

```
spontaneous  are  few  and  far  between,  but  when
you decide to do it, it certainly feels great. I
apologize if it's a bit odd for me to come here
and pour out my emotions or involve you in the
life of an 18-year-old girl whom you don't even
know personally.
```
```
Lila
```

After I returned, I sat down in front of my husband's computer, and with one finger, letter by letter, I started typing. After some time, he upgraded his computer; I took the old one, went into the laundry room, disassembled my home-based darkroom and packed everything in boxes. All the negatives engraved with precious moments on which I had toiled day after day during all my years of work were stuffed into several more boxes. Dozens of thousands of tiny rectangles that were once exposed to the light were now returning to darkness. After sealing them with thick packing tape, I wrote dates on them with a magic marker. A decade and a half of invested effort, of passion and ambition, of my own personal art, of what defined me and what I had thought of as my path in life ever since I had conscious memory, now closed in several boxes. And I moved them to my parents' storage room.

Between the washing machine and the dryer, I arranged for myself a little corner where I could write, and I promised to write every day, but my baby still wasn't sleeping through the night, and I was awake with her for hours on end. In the morning, I tried to catch up on a few hours of sleep and then run some errands, because there were always errands to run. There was shopping, and we were out of diapers, and she was sick and then he was running a fever, and at three o'clock I already had to run to bring them from the day care. She wanted to go to the park; he wanted to watch television. She ate only cheese puffs; he ate only chips. She was skinny and had to be fed; he was a bit chubby and I had to keep an eye on him so he wouldn't gobble up all the cookies. She wanted someone to push her while she sat on the swing; he wanted to jump from the highest slide straight down to the asphalt. And they both had a costume party, and there were costumes to prepare, baths to run, lice to comb out, play dates with other children because we must develop their sociability, and then, after the nightly War of Baths, one must summon up all of one's patience to complacently tell a bedtime story, with a very calm voice. And I did want to tell a story.

And I wanted to write. And every moment that I wasn't sitting in front of the computer, I dreamed of getting there, and continuing to develop my story, my characters, the women who had become my friends, who were trying to make my voice heard, and yet another day went by during which I didn't have the time to get to it. Another day went by during which there were so many things that were so much more important and urgent, and I knew that if I didn't make the time and place for it, then it wouldn't happen. I understood that I had to get some help to free myself for writing, but it seemed a bit over the top. Because it wasn't really a job. It was an experiment. It was a dream. It was something that would probably amount to nothing in the end. It wasn't a job. Because a job is something that someone pays you for.

My entire self-conception as an adult was as someone who worked, who earned, and who supported herself. I never lived on anyone else's tab. I never had to thank anyone for my food or my clothes. Now, I was someone searching for herself, who invented occupational therapy for herself, who tried to take it seriously, and knew that the chances were that she was doing something that she'd later throw in the garbage, something that wouldn't lead her anywhere. And I didn't dare indulge myself and take a nanny for several hours just so I could write, because I wouldn't allow myself to spend money on this ridiculous attempt to achieve a groundless and illogical dream, which would never really come true.

My man was wonderful, and he supported me, and he wanted me to hire someone to help me as much as possible, just so I'd be happy, but I felt stupid. I felt ridiculous. Especially next to him, because he became more and more successful, earned money, became someone and something, while I turned into something that I never thought I'd be. A housewife, a caretaker, someone lost and confused, searching for her way. Someone so remote from the person I had meant to be and was expected by myself and others to become.

Hi, Lihi.

Do you know how it is when you crave a change in life, when you find that you haven't achieved what you wanted to be when you were young? Do you know that feeling when you have everything, but deep inside you feel confused about everything? That's where I am. In ten more days, I'll be 34, and I haven't done anything with my life, except of course, create the amazing family that I've managed to raise, for which I'm grateful with every passing day. Really, I am.

But professionally speaking, I am an office manager for a CEO and I want to move on, but there's nowhere to go and no way to climb up. I don't have an academic degree. So for now, I'm sitting in the office, serving him his espresso exactly like he likes it. And I have to smile and show that everything's just great because we have to be nice, quick, thorough, sharp, and understanding. We earn a thousand dollars a month, work from eight to four, and return home happily to do our Bible homework on the Book of Joshua, which we studied for the entire term (fourth grade).

I need a change at work; I need real action; I need active assignments that will give me the energy to get up in the morning. Do you have any ideas?

Well, there you have it. I wrote and unburdened myself to a person who doesn't know me, but also doesn't silence me, and I'm sure even understands me. Thanks for listening.

Gila

# 11

*What is thy request? it shall be even given thee to the half of the kingdom.*

(Esther 5:3)

The princess is with the heiress in the morning, and runs around in the afternoon with the two heirs from one activity to another, and invites other children over to play with them. They arrive with their mothers, and they sit, a circle of mothers of toddlers and preschoolers, at each other's houses, or on the bench outside the enrichment classes, and discuss child-development issues, share information, learn from each other while wordlessly scrutinizing each other and comparing the children.

One day the princess arrives to collect the heir from preschool and the teacher calls her aside. For the past week, the heir has refused to help tidy up the blocks at cleanup time, and that certainly isn't normal behavior. They're both extremely concerned by the matter. In the afternoon, the princess arrives at the occupational therapy clinic and tells the therapist that all the other children at preschool pick up the blocks and only the heir refuses to do so. Adamantly refuses. The therapist is silent. She's also extremely concerned by this information. "And is he willing to tidy other things?" she asks, trying to extract further details concerning this

84

worrisome deviation. "Yes," the princess says in heartbreaking concern. "The truth is that this is very strange," says the therapist, and after a minute suggests giving him a present every time he tidies up the blocks at preschool. The princess heaves a sigh of relief. There's a solution. The heir is saved. She'll bribe him, and he'll behave normally.

It's her role now, the princess's, to ensure that everything continues normally with him. She knows how important it is that the heir do all the right things on time. She's responsible for his development, for molding him into who he'll grow up to be. Every compliment he receives is in fact a compliment that she receives. If he's nice and polite, it's thanks to her. If he's friendly, it's thanks to her, because she's such a wonderful mother. But if he screams and stamps his feet, or God forbid, won't pick up the blocks, it's because of her. It's her fault. She's the one who screwed up. She's read all the psychology books about child development, and she knows that she's responsible. She knows that if she doesn't teach him how to pick up the blocks on time, it could affect his entire life. She can't understand how, after all her investment, despite all the attention she gives him, this has happened.

At a certain age, he's supposed to draw a man without legs, and at a certain age he's supposed to draw a man with arms, and if a drop of black seeps into a child's drawing, well, that's that. He's a goner. She's a goner. Perhaps it has something to do with the fact that she put him in preschool too early, or too late, or because yesterday she didn't have the patience to read him a story for the third time and she told him to go to sleep already and even yelled at him that she was too tired. Or maybe because two weeks ago, when they played at home with his blocks, she picked them up for him. Because it was easier than getting into a struggle with him over the entire issue. And she knows that it is entirely unacceptable. And she decides to make more of an effort, and be more patient, because you can't turn back time, and time is so important and so significant, and she swears that she'll summon all her strength and be wonderful, because she believes that only if she is wonderful will her children be wonderful as well. Like the neighbor's children. Or even more wonderful than them. Now she's a woman raising children. It's not her happiness that's at issue here. She mustn't choose what's good for her, what makes her happier, because they're the ones who matter now. Only them.

I'm 32 years old, married, with three daughters. I was also one of those girls in class who weren't popular and weren't unpopular. I was the kind of girl who hoped that the boy I had a crush on would notice me, and I hoped that everyone would discover who I really am, and that I'm great, and I always tried to please others. Apparently, I still do. I always think that everyone is better than me, that I'm not as smart as my friend, that I haven't achieved enough for my age (is there really such a thing???).

It's unbelievable how we carry these stupid things from the past. I've achieved so much in my life. I was an officer in the army. I graduated from university successfully. I got married and have three daughters, a supportive husband, a good job, and I also look much better than I did when I was sixteen. Yet nevertheless, I'm still trying to do the right thing, and I'm still in an inferior position (if only in my thoughts), and

I'm still hoping to discover at our class reunion that the most popular girl in class turned out to be ugly.

How does one make it this far? I'm already an adult! Perhaps parents should be told to praise their children; tell them that they're beautiful and smart and that we love them unconditionally, and maybe then, they'll think the best of themselves. On the other hand, maybe they'll become spoiled rotten. Who knows?

Nili

The princess knows that every moment in which she loosens her grip or gives up or falls or screws up will come back to her later in agonizing lashes of regret. Because children remember. They remember mistakes that remain like scratches that scar their young souls. And she has to be careful to avoid that. She mustn't screw up or say the wrong thing – those things that parents do or say, and then the children carry them for years. Just like she'll never forget how her mother told her that it's a good thing she didn't get the solo dance in the ballet class because the soloist really was better than her. And that's what she's afraid of. She's afraid of becoming one of those scarring mothers, those bad mothers, inattentive, who think only about themselves, who raise children with problems and complexes that haunt them for life, who later on go to therapy for years to complain about them, about those mothers who didn't give them what they needed, exactly what they needed, and didn't notice that they were having a hard time, and didn't help them, and now, here they are, miserable because of them. And because of this fear, the princess tries to make sure that everything is as perfect as can be.

She insists on adhering to the rules. No eating in the living room; no eating in front of the television; no playing with food with your hands; no candy; toys must be returned to their proper places; no budging from the set schedule, especially before bedtime; teeth must be brushed thoroughly three times a day. And she won't neglect those things, and she'll take care of all the details. She fills their afternoons with enrichment activities because, as it is, she's in agony over all those hours during which the heir was at preschool without her to watch over him.

And when the prince once again raises the issue of their vacation, she hedges and postpones, and postpones again, because the heir really needs her now. This is exactly the stage in which he needs to feel that they believe in him, just now when he's developing rebelliousness – for example, the blocks – and neither can she leave the heiress, whom she still breast-feeds, and perhaps it's his reaction to the birth of his sister and that's what's hurting him so, and that's why he's behaving like this, and is refusing to tidy up the blocks. And even though she feels that she needs a vacation and some space, because her nerves are shot, she doesn't dare leave them, either of them, because she swore to herself to be a wonderful mother, and she won't hurt them, and she certainly won't put her needs before theirs.

But late at night, when she's alone, the princess knows the truth. He's sweet, the heir – the heir whom she tied to her chest and walked around with proudly as though she was the first mother in the world, as though she had managed to do the unbelievable, as though he's the most wonderful answer to all of mankind's ills. Yet, she also knows that he's not exactly Leonardo da Vinci, even though she bought and played for him the entire Baby Mozart series. She knows that the little heir is smart, but he also has some problems. He isn't very popular, and he also has some difficulties, and the teacher says that she has to work harder with him because in a short time he's starting the first grade, and even though he's so charming (they both agree on that), he needs more help, and perhaps he has an auditory or attention problem – many children do, but these things should be checked out, otherwise he'll have a very hard time in the first grade, because it's a serious school and it's important that he arrive prepared. The princess starts running around in order to bring him to that line, that correct line where he has to stand with all the rest, exactly the same. And she no longer wants her heir to be a genius. She just wants him to be happy, and be like everyone else. No more, no less.

And it drives her mad that he doesn't eat enough vegetables.

Only you can understand what I went through today. On Friday, all the kids were asked to dress up as characters from the Bible. My youngest (second grade) chose a brown sack that would give her an ancient appearance, a long wooden staff, and a white beard and eyebrows (she talked about this costume all day long on Saturday and was so excited). She called it "Moses." When she returned from school I asked her how it went. She said to me, "Not good. I almost fell off the stage because the sack got tangled between my legs."

I hurt for her so badly; I wanted to protect her. Had I been there, I certainly would have helped her. The mere thought almost made me cry in front of her. Because of the disappointment, the difficulty, the need to cope (I'm sure some people will laugh at me). I didn't even tell my husband because he wouldn't have understood why

I'm making such an issue out of it. And yet, how
else will they grow up? Can we always be next to
them? Can we always reach out and give them a
helping hand? It hurts…and it doesn't get easier…
Tova

One day, when I came to pick up my little girl from preschool, the
teacher called me to the side, and with a worried look in her eyes,
she told me she thought there was a problem. My daughter didn't
respond like the rest of the children. I told her that we'd noticed
that something was wrong, and we'd set up an appointment with
an ear expert. During the days that passed until the appointment,
we circled her in the house, my man and I, trying to check whether
she could hear us. We raised our voices suddenly, dropped things
on the floor, and clapped our hands behind her back. She didn't
really respond. My man tried to calm me down, I tried to calm
him, and neither of us calmed down.

The ear doctor said that he couldn't tell for sure what the
problem was, and recommended doing another examination,
this time in a hospital.

While we waited for the next appointment, going out of our
minds from worry, we started asking questions and gathering
information. With every question we asked, and every answer
we received, we became even more worried. We started to
understand that perhaps it wasn't a hearing problem. We couldn't
breathe, and late at night, before the fateful examination, my man
held me close to him, as close as he could, and I held him, and we
both shut our eyes but couldn't fall asleep. I lay down and prayed,
and vowed, and promised God everything– everything I had,
everything I could give – on condition that we'd find out that she

was deaf. Because I wanted a deaf child. *Please, God, give me a deaf child*, I begged, because all the other possibilities were much more frightening.

# 12

*He asked water, and she gave him milk;*
*she brought forth butter in a lordly dish.*

(Judges 5:25)

The princess was destined for greatness. As she was growing up, she knew exactly what she was going to be: a real superwoman, in leggings or in a ball gown wrapping her perfect body, who would float with a smile and ever so lightly amongst her beautiful, tidy children who would receive all the quality time in the world, and never watch television out of boredom but only for developmental and educational purposes. From them, she would continue floating, without ever being late, into the board meeting where everyone would be sitting with suits and laptops that projected PowerPoint presentations on the walls, and she would knock them all off their feet from enthusiasm and admiration. Her hair would always look wonderful, tidy, and blow-dried, and in the evening she'd go out, evening after evening, clubbing and dancing, and at night would become, in the blink of an eye, a wild, sexy animal, competing with all the twenty-two-year-olds with the pouty lips, and she wouldn't have extra fat anywhere, or cellulite, or wrinkles. She'd never say that she was tired, and she certainly wouldn't say that she had a headache; beneath her suit she'd wear seductive thongs, and she'd be flexible and wild enough to achieve all the things they do in porno movies, and she'd get up early the next morning singing with a happy smile on her face, like a sweet Mary Poppins, wake up the children, prepare them for day care and school, and then continue on to work, where she'd be brilliant and efficient and would never make mistakes, never miss a day because one of the children was ill, and happily do whatever she was asked to do, and her boss would be so satisfied.

However, the princess's life is now far away from that fantasy. After everything she's done, after all her studies and work and hopes and dreams, she turned into a housewife. She says to herself that it's just for the time being, but she can't stop thinking about the fact that she's not any different from the Queen Mother.

During these moments, when she's a bit disappointed, and a bit confused, and a bit far from what she thought she'd grow up to be, she reminds herself that she's doing the most important thing anyone can do. She's a mother.

And she takes the heirs to see a play. She dresses them nicely and wears her new white pants, and she's proud of herself. Here she is, the dedicated mother providing her children with a cultural experience, and when they leave the play, the heirs will be enriched; they'll be smarter and more successful than they were before they got there. She stands in the foyer of the local cultural center, looking around her at the dozens of young mothers, who at that moment – regardless of their body measurements, of what they're wearing, and of the fact that in another hour they might go out in the evening and look wonderful – all look awful to her. Grey. Hunched. Exhausted. Every one of them is coaxing her child, or children, not to scream, not to eat another ice cream, not to ask for another candy or another present from the vendor circling the area with all kinds of lame plastic made-in-China toys that he sells at exorbitant prices; to please stop eating chips, climbing, crying, and just be content for one minute. And she knows that she looks just like them. And she's behaving just like them. And in the car on the way home, when they cry over some toy or ice cream that she didn't buy them, she discovers that her white pants are smeared with stains from one of the candies she *did* buy them, and she screams at her children.

> When my youngest (now a year and a half old) was born, my oldest child was three and a half. A mommy's girl and mommy's only. Her preschool teacher told me that because I breast-fed for so long (a year and a half) my daughter is overly attached to me. Okay, I'm also very attached to her. Now she's five, a difficult age. She's a good girl, sensitive, and somewhat spoiled. When her brother was born, she was very jealous. You're probably familiar with those waves of jealousy. And I feel like this mothering business only gets harder, because not only am I not an ideal mother, I feel like a lot of the time I really don't give my all. But, what – am I not allowed to get annoyed when she dawdles before bedtime? Okay, it's not so terrible, and she does it so sweetly, but I get really angry. Or when she chatters endlessly before bath time and giving her a quick shower takes me an hour. What exactly am I so angry about? And I do get really angry. And then later, I'm angry at myself.
>
> Shayna

And the princess is mad at herself. She's mad that she's mad at her children, when they're not to blame. After all, they're only children. They're beautiful, they're sweet, they're smart; but she has to admit that they're not perfect. She tries to understand where she went wrong, what she should have done, why she doesn't have more patience, and why she explodes at them. She tries so hard, gives and provides – why isn't she succeeding? She's disappointed with herself for taking out her anger on them – her anger at her life in which she just gives all the time and never receives anything in return, her anger at feeling that she's sacrificed so much and no one seems to notice. No one seems to appreciate it. No one calls her to the victor's podium and, in an extremely majestic ceremony with numerous participants, hangs a medal on her breasts – which no longer stand high and perky inside the push-up bra after the births and breast-feeding – and tells her that what she's done is unbelievable, really unbelievable; because after all, she *has* done so much, and she deserves many thanks for all her efforts and sleepless nights, and all her running around, and her attentiveness and attention to miniscule details, and her internal conflicts.

She really *is* a champion. She wants everyone to think she deserves a medal, but she begins to understand that no one really sees all she's done. No one even notices. Especially not the prince, who doesn't grant her the thanks that she needs and craves so desperately. And suddenly she realizes that the prince doesn't even know how difficult it is for her. He thinks it's easy for her. He thinks this is what she loves to do and wants to do more than anything. Because all the princesses in all the fairy tales have filled this role so joyously and lovingly, feeling sated and content as they give, bestow, and nurture. This is the supreme goal of the good-hearted princesses in the fairy tales: to give. She also wanted to give and bestow and nurture and that's what she told her prince.

Yet, she also wanted him to appreciate what she's sacrificing, not for herself, but for both of them, for their family.

She thinks about all the fairy tales and realizes that they all end before this stage. They end with the prince and princess riding off into the sunset, and then it's just "they lived happily ever after." Fairy tales never describe how grey, exhausting, and consuming it is after the sunset. She's mad at him, at the prince. She's mad because she's fulfilling her side of the agreement, and he isn't fulfilling his. His side of the agreement is that he's supposed to cherish her and worship her, and provide her with everything. She wants the entire package promised to her. Including the castle, the horse, and the prince washing the dishes. And he must wash them joyously, not because she asked him to, but because he wants to. She doesn't want to settle for almost, or half, or a quarter of what she dreamed of, of what she was promised. Of what he promised her.

"Tell me what you want," he tells her, "and I'll do it gladly." But she doesn't want to tell him; she doesn't want to ask. She wants him to see. To see her. And he doesn't see. So she implies. With a look, with a gesture; and she makes some comments, here and there, corrects him a bit, tells him what he should have said, done, brought, remembered, forgotten. And with all her insinuations and instructions, he still doesn't do exactly what she wants him to do. Or the way she wants him to do it. And she's mad at him.

I'm on maternity leave, probably too extended (in a minute, he'll be off to university [he's a year and a half old]). I still haven't managed to find a job where I can come home at three o'clock. (How is it that I haven't received even one answer after all the resumes I sent? Doesn't anyone want a mother of two?) This week, we returned from an exhausting weekend in Eilat with the two ninjas: our eight-year-old and the baby. My husband was in shock. He kept asking if the baby cries as much at home. "No," I replied, "at home he reads books and sits with his hands folded."

After three difficult days full of yelling and crying (mine as well), he still didn't understand what I wanted him to do. After all, he works so hard all day (and now I'm at home), but I was hoping that maybe he'd just say that he feels sorry for me, and thinks that I deserve (at least) a gold medal. Of course, it was a forlorn hope. After I told him what I wanted him to say, the moment had passed. It's so easy for us to understand, and so hard for them. Why is it so hard for them? Why?! After 12 years of marriage, we probably won't stop hoping, trying, and experiencing disappointment.

P.S. This letter was written under uproarious objections, while chips were being shoved down my bra, and with the kiddie channel screaming in the background, all under the patronage of the little ninja. Help.

Tammy

The prince tries very hard to make her happy, but whatever he does, it never satisfies her. It's never exactly as she'd like, and most of the time it even just annoys her. When he buys her something, she exchanges it. When he suggests they go out to a movie, she's too tired. He tries to listen more and understand more, and still nothing works. He begins to be afraid to even try. He fears that perhaps he'll never manage to give her just what she wants, the way she wants it, exactly when she wants and with the right words and facial expressions to make her happy.

The prince recalls how once upon a time, she, his princess, looked at him with adoring round doe eyes, and laughed at things he said, and was happy with everything that he bought her; and he hopes that one day, he'll be able to make her happy. Maybe then, the joyous sparkle will return to her eyes, and she'll simply be happy that she has him. He, who had dragon-high fantasies, who believed that his princess would never grow old, never gain weight, and would forever remain sweet, graceful, and full of life, no longer dares to fantasize about the simplest thing in the world: coming home from work and sharing with her that he had a difficult day, without her immediately telling him that she had it harder. He no longer dares to expect that when he opens the front door she'll be genuinely happy to see him; that they'll laugh together again, go out on a date together, that she'll really want to have sex tonight. That she'll initiate it. That maybe she'll even have several daring ideas. But she's tired, and the kids have already pestered her so, and the sink is packed with dishes that have to be put in the dishwasher, and once again, he forgot to fix the dripping faucet. He no longer hopes to return home and be welcomed by a smiling princess, or that there'll be that old twinkle of appreciation in her eye, let alone adoration. When he returns home from another day of work, all he hopes for is that just this once, today, just today, she won't be so angry with him. She won't be so disappointed in him, again.

Without even noticing, he starts searching for detours. Paths that will bypass the togetherness that is his and hers, trying to postpone the moment of their meeting, the moment when he'll come face to face with that look, or receive a scolding for something truly shocking that he did, such as failing to notice that his towel fell on the floor. Before he enters his castle in the evening, he finds himself standing by the front door for a moment. A moment in which he inhales deeply, trying to postpone the encounter between them for just another second. Postpone the moment when she'll explain to him that he's in the wrong, again.

> It's so great to know that everyone goes through the same things (even though you have two kids and I have only one, 11 months old). We've only been married for two years, but it feels to me like ten at least. I guess it's only the beginning of all the arguments and the power struggles. How do you stay married to the same person for 20-30 years and more (like our parents) — how?!? I have no idea. We'll see how long we last — if we last.
>
> Dahlia

The prince and the princess, who just several years ago promised to walk down the path of life together, to support, to help, to be friends and to share their dreams, suddenly discover, each on their own, that they're no longer one being. Each of them is now carrying his or her own baggage on their backs; each of them is coping with his or her difficulties alone. Each of them is walking down a different path. There's no longer *their* desires, *their* hopes, *their* needs. Their goals are so different that they can't even see the needs of the other, or how hard the other one is trying. He's coping alone. And she's coping alone. Some of their needs even turn them against each other. Him against her and her against him. And neither of them remembers when they last sat down with each other, just for the fun. Or the pleasure. Or when they laughed together. When they got a hug. When they received encouragement, support, or appreciation. There are too many struggles, complaints, and reinforced silences in their encounters. And their bed is more full of children than sex.

# 13

*And she sat over against him,*
*and lift up her voice, and wept.*

(Genesis 21:16)

The examination concluded that the little one wasn't deaf.

We sat with her on the bench outside the hospital, holding each other, trying to absorb, trying to breathe, and the tears silently streamed from my eyes. I understood that until this moment, I hadn't known the meaning of pain.

> I'm known as a person who has ants in her pants. I've always searched for ways to break out of the routine. Almost every day had to hold in store an adventure, or some form of entertainment or meeting, so it wouldn't be boring. The years, the children, and life have taught me (just recently) how blessed is the routine.
>
> Ayelet

My man and I decided to fight. To fight that dragon. *We're the kind of people who don't give up*, we said; *we'll do everything and save her.* We'd do everything. We'd raise hell. We divided the roles between us. He inquired and investigated the methods with which we could treat her, and wrote and called people all around the world, and questioned experts about new methods of treatment, and each person said something else and no one could say exactly what we had to do. And each expert had his own way, and what he believed in, and a new study was published every day, with new promises, and we had to decide. We constantly had to make decisions, and choose who to believe, and which path to pursue. I ran with her to appointments and evaluations and tried to understand exactly what she had, and what it was going to look like, and what the future held in store for us, and what hope we had. And here as well, every expert said something else.

One day, I went to spy on her at the preschool, and she was standing at the gate and staring out. And after several hours, I went down to buy something at the supermarket, and she was still there, still staring out. It was obvious that we couldn't leave her in preschool anymore. And from the next day she didn't go there anymore. From that moment she was at home with us. We didn't have the advantage of time on our side, which was another aspect that we had to fight, because as long as she was young, there was a good chance for improvement, for progress. We ran with her to more and more assessments and consultations. And during all that time, she hardly slept at all. Barely four hours a day. And we had to keep an eye on her every second, every minute, all the time, because she could climb, and run up and down, and pull and pour and dump things out, and that was the role that I assumed. I was in charge of the house, which in an instant had become her house. A house that revolved around her only.

We had to bring in experts from abroad, and find people in the country who knew what to do. And we found teachers and brought experts to teach the teachers, and she was at home all the time. And there were treatments, and the house was always full of people and resembled a train station, and there wasn't even one moment of privacy. And all this needed funding, and my man took this upon himself. "Don't worry about it," he said, and took that burden on his shoulders, and took care of it, promising himself and me that he'd bring her the moon if that was what she needed. And I supervised all the time. Every second and every minute. Examined what exactly they were doing with her, and how, and what we hadn't done yet, and what we still hadn't tried. And we knew that we couldn't count on anyone. Only on ourselves. So we did the most important thing: we fought for her, and I knew that never before in my life had I done anything as important. And I wasn't interested in what was happening around me in the world, because the entire world had been sucked into a fog. I wasn't interested in anything. Only one thing was clear to me. I was the mother of my child. And I had to save her.

# 14

*Two, the male and his female.*

(Genesis 7:2)

The prince arrives home from another hard day at work, this time early enough, while the heirs are still awake, and he tells them a story, and then joins the princess in the living room. They sit together. The house is sparkling clean, and she's prepared a delicious meal, and they chat a bit, for the first time in a long while. He tells her what happened to him today at work, and who he saw, and what sort of problems he came across. And she's so happy, even though she isn't familiar with most of the names, and even though she doesn't have an opinion concerning most of his dilemmas; she's just happy that they're talking and sharing.

Then she tells him about her day. About something that the preschool teacher said about the heir, something that someone told her this afternoon in the park, and about the lady who stood on line at the supermarket, in the express line, with two items more than the limit. "The nerve," she says to the prince. "Wasn't it rude of her?"

And he's silent.

He maintains that silence of his. A silence that she also maintains sometimes. And these silences, which settle between their sentences, stretch and take over, marking the widening gap between them. The gap between what interests them, between what they need, what they want, what they give. A silent testimony that he isn't really interested in what is happening to her, in what she's going through, and he isn't really interested in sharing his world with her, and she isn't genuinely interested in his world. This silence has always annoyed her, but this time it's different. Maybe because she isn't tired, because she snatched a few hours of sleep in the morning, she isn't annoyed this time. This time, something else happens to her. Suddenly she sees herself.

After years during which she has examined the world only through the lens of what seems important to her – her difficulties, her efforts to make her little family perfect and their children wonderful – suddenly she sees herself as though she's looking in from the outside. She sees herself through different eyes. Suddenly she's aware of herself, sprawled on the couch. How she no longer makes sure that her chin is coquettishly extended, and how she's neglected her hair like never before, how she's wearing rags, and without even checking, she knows that she has hair on her legs.

And not only does she suddenly see herself, she also hears herself. Hears what she was talking about, what her life revolves around, how her world has narrowed down to their neighborhood, and who said what to whom, and that the highlight of her day was that rude lady in the supermarket. (Actually, there was another highlight when she found that soup pot she's been wanting at a crazy discount.) And it frightens her. She imagines a young her, a twenty-something-year-old, sitting with them right now, with all her passion, and thinks what her younger self would have to say if she were looking at her now. The princess she used to be wanted to swallow life, eat it, dance with it, climb all its heights, confront all its dangers, touch all its flames. And now, here it is, her life, sprawled like a rag on the couch, silent and small. As distant as the distance between fairy tales and real life. And she knows that the princess she once was wouldn't have let it happen. She swore that it wouldn't happen to her, that she wouldn't surrender to this game, that she'd fight the story's confines and change the end. Because she believed in happily ever after even after the story ended.

Now, it seems so far away. And she also seems so far away, from her life and from herself, from what she hoped and swore she'd be. And her heart aches because she knows that she's disappointed herself, the young princess she once was. And she knows that had her younger self been here and seen her now, she would have dismissed her as a total sell-out. Because she turned into everything she swore her entire life not to be. She's a woman crushed under the wheels of a truck bringing fresh rolls to the supermarket.

And she knows, at that exact moment, that she is no longer a princess. She has become a queen. A queen like all those fairy tale queens. A queen who's obsessed with the little details, who's mad at the entire world – a cranky, sour queen, with a face that has lines of bitterness distorting the corners of her mouth with a twist that can turn even the prettiest face into an ugly one. A queen who's angry that her glory, beauty, and youth have withered.

So she stretches a bit, sits up, straightens her posture, and runs her fingers through her hair, tousling it mischievously. But the prince has already turned on the television.

I have two children, thank God. I didn't want to have any more. Work, running about, and life in general... My husband really wanted more kids, and

I enjoyed his courtship and pleas for another child. I enjoyed the control over my body and my spouse. I always promised that after I finished one more thing that I hadn't yet achieved, then we'd have another child. At the age of 35, I was diagnosed with cancer.

Never mind the physical and mental agony. I knew that now I'd never have another child. I didn't know if I should feel sorry for my husband or for myself. I'd pay a fortune for a baby to wake me up at night, to interrupt me in the middle of whatever I'm trying to get done, smear the house with chocolate, scatter the Legos around the house, force me to drop everything at four o'clock in order to pick him up and take him to his afternoon activities.

Please enjoy your children, because it never returns. And yearning for it just unsettles you. Now, I'm 38 years old. I have a 19-year-old daughter and a 13-year-old son, and I feel old. And with my husband, there are many silences.

Mona

I was angry. Terribly angry. Angry with God for hurting my child, who never hurt anyone. I was angry with the people walking down the street. I was angry at the world that continued as though nothing had happened, as though the sky hadn't fallen. I was angry at the fact that not everyone stopped, not everything came to a standstill in the face of this sin, this punishment that this little girl, this gentle and heartbreakingly beautiful child, had to endure. The whole time I was pregnant with her, I thought that since her brother had inherited my blue eyes from me, she probably wouldn't. I was positive that she wouldn't have blue eyes. But she did have blue eyes, because God really did make her beautiful. More beautiful than anyone else.

Why did He do that? Why didn't He forego the sweet nose, the blue eyes? Why the hell did He have to ruin it in the end? Why couldn't He sit for one more minute, one more second, and do what was truly important? I was terribly angry with Him. With God. And with the world. I was angry that you could send a man to the moon, and there were satellites, that someone had solved the mystery of atoms, that there's such a thing as a fax, that humanity has done so much and evolved so much and knows so much, and no one can teach my child to say "Mommy."

■ ■ ■

The princess looks at the prince, at his profile, when he's looking at the screen that flickers and paints him in cold, artificial colors, and she sees that the years have left their mark on him. She sees his receding hairline. His little paunch. And suddenly he looks like an adult. A man. And she remembers her prince from long ago. She remembers how handsome she thought he was, and how he excited her, and how she loved to lean her head in the hollow between his shoulder and neck, where she felt safe, and where she felt loved, and how just one single look, and one single smile, made her feel like nothing bad could happen to her. And she misses him. She misses who she used to be, and who they used to be, and their togetherness. She feels like extending her hand and inviting him to run away together. She has this wild impulse to ask him to leave everything, take the kids with them, and travel, travel without a plan, to the big world that lies outside. Without a thing, they don't need a thing, only a backpack: Africa,

South America, forget everything. No more carpooling, no more cleaning, no more cooking, just lounging together on a distant beach, far away in the Far East, barefoot.

But she doesn't dare say it. He'll think she's gone crazy, that she's lost her mind. She knows what an obligation he has to the kingdom, and the debts that they have to pay. And she couldn't do it to his parents or to hers. They're not twenty-year-olds; they're adults with obligations and commitments, and there is no place in their lives for crazy fantasies.

And as the lights and voices continue blaring out of the television, she realizes that they're no longer building the foundations of their future. This is their future. This is her life, their life, and it's not something on the way to somewhere.

This is her husband, these are her children, and this is her. Now, she's at that part of the story that arrives after the climax. After the sunset. That part of the story that no one bothers to write. That no one bothers to tell. The part that comes after. After the end. And after the end, she knows, there isn't much chance that anything exciting will happen. Because this isn't the exciting part of the story, of life. And she hopes that he'll see the tear that falls silently on her cheek, and hopes that he'll say something.

She remembers all those times that he offered to take her on a romantic vacation, just the two of them, and how she refused. And after so long that she hasn't felt this way, she wants him to hug her, to run his hands over her lustfully, like he used to, just so she can remember how she used to feel. She knows that it won't happen. Because that's not how they do it. Only when they go to sleep, when both of them are in bed, does he reach for her. She's refused him too many times. She's said yes too few times, and when she said yes, there were too many times that she said yes just because there were too many times that she'd already said no. And she knows that he'd be happy if she made the first move, but she no longer remembers how to do it. And she no longer remembers how to want it. And she can't find the words. And she doesn't know how to suggest. They've been role-playing for so long, playing a game in which he wants and she doesn't, in which he is silent and she is upset. In which he is disappointed and she is disappointed too. And there is silence. And the only voices heard are blaring from the television.

Every woman I meet, who has less than a minute to talk, deals with the exact same issues and complains about them. I've been a nurse for 18 years. Occasionally, I let off a load of complaints about work, about my children, and about the obvious – my husband, may he live a long life (yes, sometimes I'm not opposed to his staying alive and I even want him to).

Yesterday, I was at the emergency room and a woman with frightened eyes and a baby in her arms arrived. Her husband went up to fix something on the roof and fell from a great height. I think that all she wanted at that moment was to return to her boring routine, to a husband lounging on the sofa (the husband who isn't exactly the friend and lover that she wished for), to the children screeching in the living room.

I see tragedies every day, and it puts things into perspective. This morning, I called all my belligerent girlfriends and told them that they should say a prayer of thanks every day, three times a day, for almost everything and especially

for what they take for granted. It's a shame
that we need a tragedy in order to know how to
appreciate things.

Daphna

Twice a week, we went with our little girl to a place where they treated children like her. There, we met parents like ourselves. Parents who, one sunny day, had a block of concrete fall on their heads, and they, like us, didn't know how to carry on. Apart from my man, these were the only people who understood how I felt. In this entire world, out of all the people with whom I was previously acquainted, who mainly had no idea what to say, who saw my pain but were helpless and tried not to look into my eyes, these were the only people who understood. The only people who were as angry as I was. Who were as lost as myself. And I wanted to be only with them. Because I wanted to talk about it. Especially with the mothers. And I held on to them. And these days with them were what kept me afloat. Just like the group of mothers in the park had kept me afloat when the children were tiny. Because I could talk to them. Because they understood. And I held on to the group with all the strength I had in my ragged nails. And I waited for these meetings like a person waits for oxygen.

Once every two weeks, we, the parents, met at a support group. One time, the facilitator started the meeting by suggesting that we not talk about the children. That we talk about our hobbies. A silence descended on the room. A terrible silence. It was the most inappropriate offer, in the most inappropriate place, at the worst moment of our lives. A moment in which none of us remembered if we had ever even had hobbies. Or remembered if we had ever done something for ourselves that didn't include survival. I felt my blood boil with fury; I felt as though in another minute I'd explode on all the walls, and especially on the facilitator's head. And I couldn't keep silent. I yelled that we didn't have hobbies anymore. Because it didn't matter what we had before; now we were one thing only. I was one thing only. I was the mother of an autistic child.

Suddenly, without understanding how or why, we all burst into a crazy, huge laughter. All the parents there laughed. We laughed for the first time. And then we started going out together in the evenings. Once a week, we went out, to laugh together, to cry together. And apart from those evenings, I didn't laugh at all. For a very long time.

# 15

*Wash thyself therefore, and anoint thee,*
*and put thy raiment upon thee...*

(Ruth 3:3)

The prince's work announces a big event for the employees on the occasion of a change of CEOs. The prince tells the princess about the party, and knowing her, he immediately adds that he knows that she doesn't have the patience for these events, and he'll understand if she doesn't feel like going. But the princess says that she'll be glad to come. *He reacted to that somewhat strangely,* she thinks to herself the next morning, *not very happily,* as though he's a bit disappointed that she wants to come. And it confuses her. He's always expressed such a desire that she come with him to company events, always pleaded with her, and it's true that most of the time she stayed at home and he said that he didn't mind going alone, that he's used to it by now, but he always has much more fun when she comes along. She's probably mistaken, she soothes herself. He was simply surprised by the joy and exuberance with which she jumped at the opportunity. Then she scolds herself; she shouldn't have shown him how eager she was. That's what confused him – that she wasn't subtle about how much she wanted to go.

And she really does want to go, because ever since that evening in the living room she's been doing a lot of thinking about them and about herself. About what she's turned into. She decides that it's about time she get out of her sweatpants, and for the last few days she's been chopping herself a finely cut salad, hasn't touched her children's potato chips, and hasn't finished the meatballs that they left on their plates. She remembers the gym subscription that she signed up for and decides that she'll renew it at the first available opportunity. She decides that she's going to stun them all at the party.

> We read, we internalized, and this is what came out of it: yesterday evening, while the sea was high, us girls went out to celebrate International Women's Day (even though we're Israelis and not international). We decided to exceed the boundaries of stupid behavior considered legal for mature adult women like ourselves – and of course, the more stupid we were, the more we felt liberated and alive. Since we *are* women, we decided to start the evening at the mall and tried on clothes. After that, we raided the cosmetics counters, and then we continued to a club. At the Whisky a Go Go Club they didn't want to let all of us in, so we went to Shablul Jazz Club. The level of frivolity increased with the level of alcohol, which made the evening more enjoyable.
>
> So we didn't burn our bras and didn't grow mustaches, but we made a statement that we're here. To whom? Mostly to ourselves, because in life's race, amongst the diapers, homework, and gourmet cooking, sometimes we forget that we can have fun, just us girls. And that sometimes we need to be alone. Thank you.
>
> Gabi

During her not so distant youth, the princess did it so easily. All it required was another tiny effort, to wear high heels that added the desired inch, and to fix up her hair. She could enter any room and cause all eyes to turn to her. The prince would put his hand on her shoulder, with proud ownership, as if saying, *she's mine, eat your hearts out.* And she plans to make that tiny effort that she hasn't made for a long time. So she hops over to the nearest mall. She tries on clothes and takes them off, and tries on more, and after several exhausting hours, she goes back home. The next day, she goes to the mall again, this time to a different mall, and once again, she tries on clothes, and every dress or shirt that she throws on the floor pains her. In the afternoon, she goes down to the gym and asks if she can renew the subscription that she froze several years ago. They are gracious and agree on condition that she add a token payment.

The day before the company event, she goes to wax her legs and mustache and have her eyebrows plucked. On the day of the event she goes to the hairdresser, has a pedicure, manicure, and highlights. And when the prince comes home, he remembers for the first time in a very long while how pretty she is. How pretty she can be. "You look wonderful," he tells her, and can't make up his mind if he should tell her that the dress she's wearing is a bit too glittery, because he knows the women with whom he works, and knows that they'd never wear something so glittery, and certainly won't come with long dresses. He decides not to say anything, because he likes the way she looks, like a princess, and he doesn't want to say or do anything to ruin her rare good mood. The few times she's come with him to his office parties, she sat with a bored and sour expression and didn't even try to get to know or befriend anyone, and he's pleased that this time she's made such an effort.

When they arrive at the event, everyone is happy to see the prince, and casually shakes her hand and coolly says, "Pleased to meet you," and in a matter of seconds, they surround him, and his hand leaves hers, and she's left standing there, alone. She gazes around and sees all the other women, who have just thrown something on themselves, and casually wipes her face in order to rub off some of the makeup on her face, trying to erase her exaggerated efforts. If only she could tear off, one by one, the sequins that decorate her neckline, which in the dressing room illuminated her face with a glow, and now look as cheap as confetti. The prince, who stands several steps from her, is encircled by people who chat and laugh with him, and she remembers how she used to love it that people always tried to get close to him and loved him without him having to lift a finger for it. And she can see how much they like him, and how all of them, the women as well, touch him, slap him on the shoulder, laugh at what he says, whisper secrets in his ear, and he laughs that big laugh of his. The laugh that turns his eyes into two narrow slits of warmth. A warmth that has always drawn people to him so they could bask in it, in that laughter that she thought, especially during recent years, was a bit too loud and coarse.

And that man whom she saw only several days ago by the cold light of the television suddenly looks not so tired, and not so gray, but just a little older. And she stands there, immobile and glittery, and doesn't know what to do with her hands. She realizes that she doesn't know a thing about these people with whom he spends his nights and days, and that she hasn't even heard most of their names, and certainly can't make the connection between their faces and their titles, and is confused by the fact that her prince is encompassed by an entire world that loves and appreciates him.

And is interested in him. And he's interested in them. And she discovers that she is unraveling a thread from the cheap evening purse that she bought to match the dress. And the fact that it is such a perfect match mortifies her.

The host of the evening calls everyone to sit down, and the prince searches for her with his eyes and with a big smile, he leads her to their table, and briefly introduces her to everyone. She nods and knows that she won't remember even one name, even if she tries, because she is making such an effort to nod charmingly and hold in her stomach that she can't breathe. To the sound of wild applause, the new CEO gets up onstage, and her prince yells something and everyone there laughs, and she remembers how he used to make her laugh once. She tries to imagine him standing there on the stage, and she knows that he could have been the one standing there, but he isn't pushy enough, he didn't fight hard enough, didn't really comprehend office politics, those that she understands without words. Perhaps had she helped him a bit more, he would have been promoted faster. And she remembers all those times that she tried to tell him something, and how he didn't listen, and it pains her.

When the food arrives, everyone around the table chats and argues, and talks about work matters, and gossips about the people sitting around the other tables. And she sits there, a polite princess smile frozen on her face, and doesn't say a word. She doesn't have anything to contribute or say. And then someone approaches her and says, "Pleased to meet you," and tells her that she's new on her husband's team and she's so happy to finally meet her. The princess is surprised by how young and pretty she is. And then the new girl asks the princess what she does. The princess says that she has little children and that she's at home with them.

The young woman says, "Sorry, I didn't know that you just recently gave birth. He didn't say a word."

And the princess mumbles that her youngest is already four years old but she still needs her.

And the new girl says that she's sure she does, and that it was fun meeting her, and moves along.

I'm 33 years old, married with three kids. I have my weekly custom: Friday evening, after my children go to sleep, I allow myself to overeat a bit and read your column. Right now, I'm getting my driver's license. I'm having a hard time with the theory. I've flunked five theory exams. I'm desperate. I'm tired of studying. I can't open the theory book anymore. My husband helps me, my driving teacher sits with me, but then I go to the licensing office and feel as though my head is about to explode, get nervous, and flunk. I wanted to ask if you have a tip for me about how I should approach the entire matter.

And here's something for you. A recipe for a wonderful chocolate cake. Four eggs, a cup of oil, a cup of sugar, a cup of flour, a teaspoon of baking powder, a cup of cocoa, half a carton of cream. Mix all the ingredients. You can use a large spoon; you don't have to use the mixer. Preheat the oven to 350°F and bake. For the chocolate frosting, you need half a carton of cream, three and a half ounces of dark (semisweet) chocolate. Heat in a pot until it melts and pour it on the cake while it's hot.

Abigail

My man, who saw me being sucked into a maelstrom of grief and anger, spinning inside it without even attempting to break out, without believing that I could climb out, tried to save me from sinking even deeper. He stood there for me, and for our little family, like a steady rock of strength, which he drew from God knows where, and insisted that we try to move forward. That we continue with our lives, do things that couples and families do; he wanted to go on trips, go out, be happy. He wanted me to be happy. He insisted on trying to explain to me that there is a meaning to life. He tried to take me on vacations, just the two of us, so that we could preserve the wonderful thing that we once had, that was only ours, and belonged just to the two of us. Because during those lone moments in which he managed to take me away, and when we were alone, even for an hour, we loved each other so much. But there were only these lone moments, because I didn't want more. And I wouldn't let him.

I didn't want to enjoy myself. I couldn't understand how I could. Or why I should. Or what was the point of it all. I wanted to sacrifice, to give myself, all of myself, as if only by suffering I could help. I didn't want to think about myself. I didn't want to be happy. And I didn't want to go away. I wanted us to be by our daughter all the time, checking, supervising, because maybe a miracle would occur, and maybe I'd notice something. I was afraid that if I wasn't by her side for one minute, something awful would happen. Something that I'd regret later for the rest of my life. That would scar her. I wouldn't be there and someone wouldn't understand her. And she'd withdraw even more into herself. But in the meantime I withdrew into myself, into my sorrow, entrenched in my pain, unable to see a thing except my hurt.

In a pathetic attempt to reward my man, who tried to protect me and our family, and make me happy, I tried to spare him the knowledge of how miserable I was. How sad and hurt I was, and how I didn't know how to continue.

And neither of us was very successful. He knew how miserable I was, and I couldn't find a reason for joy.

■ ■ ■

The princess can't stop thinking about the party. She remembers the women there, their lightness, their smiles, their wild laughter, the confidence with which they walked, and the looks that they sent her prince. They looked at him as she no longer can. She knows too much about him. She knows the snorting sounds that he emits at night, his nose-blowing in the mornings, how he pulls in his stomach when he tries to look better, and the smell in the toilet after he leaves it. And he knows too much about her, as well. He sees the tampon wraps in the garbage, the razor that she uses to shave her armpits, the stretch marks on her stomach, her smell when she sweats. She remembers how that young woman looked at him, and that condescending and cheeky look comes back and bothers her and stabs her. But it's also her wake-up call. It makes her realize that she's not the only one who sees herself as some sort of discarded leftover. Others see her like that as well.

One evening, it's her turn to host the girls' night out, and they arrive, all her girlfriends, all of those who never stop, who keep constantly moving on in the race, working and growing. One is a psychologist, one is a doctor, and one is a teacher. Without even noticing, they scatter around stories of success, of achievements, of failures, of struggles, of an exciting life, of wild, unapologetic shopping sprees that they don't have to justify to anyone, of exhilarating trips abroad, and all the while they compliment her on her lovely palace, her tidy children, and her tasty dishes. Compliments that until recently were her adequate compensation, a source of pride and satisfaction, a sense of achievement and success, and suddenly seem to her like empty shells. This palace, which she licks clean, the children whom she nurtures, the dishes that she cooks – all these things that she puts her heart and soul into, that she dedicates all her time to – suddenly seem so unimportant.

Yes, okay, the house is clean, there's hot food, and the children are attended to, but they don't seem much happier than her friends' children. And not much more successful than them. She, who had no less potential than them, if not more, who was supposed to prance around the world wearing designer gowns, who was supposed to buy whatever she felt like buying, who was destined for greatness and success, is now receiving compliments on her clean house. On her cooking. And now, these compliments of theirs insult her. Anger her. She feels as though she doesn't deserve compliments. She hasn't achieved anything unique; she knows that each and every one of her friends could have a house like this, were they sitting at home all day and licking it clean. And she can no longer lie to herself. She can no longer say to herself that she's happy. That she's content. That she's doing the most important thing in the world.

> Can it be that we've really reached a stage in which everything is more important than myself? After ten years of marriage and two children, I can barely understand what I want. And even when I express the slightest interest in something a little bit unusual, it always scares me to try.
>
> Betty

On Saturday, I was at my parents' place. It was just another Saturday like so many other Saturdays, when I showed up in sweatpants and slippers so I could crash there. So I could tune out. It was my sanctuary and my shelter. A place where I could analyze for hours every sliver of progress, and remain silent when there were regressions. A place where my son was a king because my mother was completely overwhelmed by her love for him. A place where my wonderful father, who was connected to his granddaughter with all his soul, always had the strength to go out with her, lift her on his shoulders, encourage her, and gather the mess she left behind her, spilling, breaking, tearing to shreds the pages from the precious books organized on the shelf. The only place where I could go to sleep peacefully knowing that someone else would worry. The only place where I didn't have to hide, run after her and cover, explain, and apologize. The only place where I could cry.

That Saturday, I cried in my father's arms, and for the first time I dared ask him why.

Why did it have to happen to my baby girl?

And he was silent, and then he told me that there wasn't a better place in the world for her than with us, and that no one understood her like we did.

And then he said something that I'll never forget. He said that this is probably my role in life.

And I knew that he was right.

And he also said that I was a wonderful mother.

And that was the first time. Five and a half years after I became a mother. For five and a half years all I had done was take care of everyone, and worry, and give, and I wasn't interested in anything but my children; and for four years nothing had interested me but my daughter, and all I had felt was sorrow and anger. And now for the first time, I felt that I wasn't a failure. That maybe I was even doing okay. That I was a pretty good mother.

And it was the first time that I realized that I was crushed. That I was shattered.

If my life were a movie, I'd dismiss it on account of implausibility and excessive melodrama. The reason that I'm writing to you isn't completely clear to me. I've been thinking about taking up writing, because I want to write about what I'm going through, but I don't know how to begin. I'm intimidated by the blank page.

I'm 33 years old and I have two daughters. The oldest is four years old. She's an amazing and mature child who was diagnosed with a rare blood disease at the age of eight months. Her immune system attacks the blood cells and destroys them. She's treated with medication that suppresses the immune system, and therefore can't go to preschool and is at home, with me. Needless to say, I've left my job. We're at the hospital two to three times a week. Our entire life has been disrupted and instead of the calm mother I used to be, I've become a stressed and anxious one.

After many deliberations and consultations with doctors all over the world, we've decided on a bone marrow transplant donated from her sister - a difficult decision that the doctors placed on our shoulders. One month ago, a few weeks before the intended transplant, unbelievably, I was diagnosed with breast cancer. I had surgery

and now I'm supposed to start chemotherapy and
radiation treatments.

That's basically the whole story. What
a world. Several weeks ago I couldn't stop
complaining to my friends and husband how sick
I am of spending all my time in the hospital,
and now I'll probably spend twice as much time
there. I was also bothered by the question of
how I'd tell my daughter that her hair will fall
out, and now I can give her a live demonstration.
Currently, the transplant is on hold, because a
person can't cope with so much all at once, and
I'm just trying to remain sane and draw strength
from God knows where.

I'd appreciate it if you could give me some
advice about writing.

Yael

I was thinking about what the group facilitator asked us. About
hobbies. And I remembered that once, I had dreams. Not just
about children. Not just about my baby girl. Once, before
everything came crashing down. Before nights turned into days.
Before teachers filled the house and worked with her in her
room and my man and I sat on the other side of the closed door,
listening to her cry, torn apart by how difficult it is for her, and I
curled up in the circle of my beloved man's embrace wanting to
scream, and wanting only to wake up from this nightmare. And
I remembered that before all of this, before this dizzying cycle of
awful exhaustion and anger and heart-wrenching sorrow, I had
dreams about myself. Dreams that I hadn't dared dream for a long
time. That I was ashamed to dream. Because how could I even

dare to want something for myself when I was supposed to think only about her? And I started realizing that if I didn't have dreams to escape to, I would fall apart.

# 16

## *Wherefore she went forth out of the place where she was...*

(Ruth 1:7)

I decided to resume working on my book. And I tried to find the time to write. Like tiny shards of a smashed crystal goblet, I gathered my time, assembling piece after piece. Another sentence, another paragraph, erasing one sentence, struggling with myself, between my desire to sleep and my desire to write, trying to make up for my sleep deprivation, while briefly napping in the waiting rooms in the occupational and speech therapists' clinics, collapsing, stealing half an hour here and fifteen minutes there, and I felt like an escaped criminal. I felt as though these moments during which I sat at the computer, conversing with the characters from the book, living their lives and not mine, were an escape. An escape to a tiny, secluded island, where there is a different set of rules, where there isn't constant pain and there isn't any sorrow. Because there, in front of the computer, in the laundry room, with the monotonous sound of the washing machine cutting me off from the confusion and noise all around, I could tune out a bit. But the island was small and I barely found the time to escape to it.

After more than a year of collecting the minutes and seconds, I completed what I had once begun before my world fell apart, and I held in my hand something that looked like a book. I sent it out to a publishing house. After a month, I called them and they still hadn't read it. Two weeks later, I called again, and they still hadn't read it. Four months passed and they still didn't give me an answer. For months I checked my messages every few hours, crossed my fingers, jumped every time the phone rang, and then, I finally received an answer from the publishing house to which I had sent my book.

They said that they weren't interested. Thanks, but no thanks.

And something happened to me that hadn't happened in a long time. My heart started beating again. My veins swelled. Because I believed in it, in this book, and I wasn't prepared to give up, and I wasn't prepared to listen, and suddenly I had ambition and I remembered this feeling. This feeling that there's something I can win at. Something achievable. After so long, I felt something similar to the feeling of life. And I yelled that they're idiots, that they don't understand, that they're making a mistake. Finally, my story had a bad guy. I had someone to be mad at. I had an enemy. I had someone I had to defeat in battle and there was a chance that I'd win.

> I wanted to share something and say that during these last months, since the birth of my second son, I have finally started believing that I am allowed to enjoy, and not only to sacrifice for my home, husband, and wonderful (and demanding) children. I have just returned to myself, to moments that are just for me, even though they are supposedly "at the expense of" my loved ones. I have to mention that my husband constantly urged me to have fun and take some time for myself.

He claimed that it would be better for everyone
involved. I didn't believe him. He was right.

I hate being wrong.

But this time it's a pleasure.

P.S. My mother, a chronic sacrificer, finally
divorced my father this year, and she's at the
height of her glory and joy of life. This divorce
proved to me that every person or subjugated
people will eventually revolt. No doubt about it.

Shelly

When the princess tidies her house, after her friends leave, she knows that she wants to do something. To be someone besides the one taking care of everyone all the time. She never thought that she'd be a full-time wife and mother. That's not why she studied. She's capable of much more. She wants to be something. She feels that if she goes out to work, she'll find her place again. At home as well. A place of respect. Of appreciation. And she wants that appreciation from the people surrounding her. Most of all, she wants it from him. From the prince. She wants him to look at her like he looked at those women at the party. The women who work with him. And she also wants to earn money. Because these conversation that they have, she and the prince, every few months, about her expenses, always leave her somewhat embarrassed, and sometimes even humiliated.

One evening, the princess notifies the prince that she wants to go back to work. The prince turns off the television and looks at her, surprised. "But it's so hard for you to manage everything and you're so tired."

And he's worried. As it is, she's so exhausted all the time, tense and nervous. She's liable to have a nervous breakdown if the heir spills some ketchup down his shirt or the heiress is five minutes late for her ballet class. How can she even think of adding work to all this? He imagines an entire new world of complaints about to crash down on him, and now she'll probably want him to help out even more at home and he was barely coping with all the stress at work, with all the dismissal letters flying around, beheading various employees. And he feels as though he can't breathe.

"Yes," she says, "but the children have grown up and I have time in the mornings."

And she also says that the money she'd earn would help them.

I wanted to tell you that there's a different kind of poverty. A quiet poverty that doesn't come across well on television. You'd see a person suffering from this kind of poverty in a soup kitchen only as a volunteer. This kind of poor person wears jeans bought in second-hand shops, and smiles, and wears her teenage daughter's outgrown sneakers, and smiles. And goes out to work and returns to a tiny rented house (500 square feet of father, mother, and two teenage daughters) in a green setting that raises new generations of salt of the earth.

This is a poverty that starts because the industrious, hard-working parents really didn't receive any help, and thanks only to waitressing, cleaning, and babysitting, managed to graduate. And back then, the smile was genuine, with a mouth full of teeth and dimples full of hope. This is a type of poor person who has been working every single day, from the age of 14, and finds time for volunteering. And has never asked for a favor, or a donation, or help, and who is now collapsing.

Fifteen years of love and marriage have passed by, during which anniversaries weren't celebrated; and so many debts have been paid off, yet we don't have a house of our own. And it seems as though we'll never have one. And it's true that we celebrate the shedding of a leaf in the fall, and the first rain, and we smile and love.

So that's how it is: a father, mother, two girls, and a cat, and with the approaching New Year holiday at the end of the week, I'm afraid that I won't have it in me to give the little extra push that will help them study without any concerns, that will enable them to learn how to dance or play a musical instrument, my two wonderful and talented teenage daughters. And I'm so scared that a day will come when I won't be able to work and won't be able to pay the rent.

I didn't think that this was how things would work out. And maybe the good Lord did forget me, or maybe He's just very busy because there are the ill and the orphaned and there are always people worse off. I thought that at the age when the dimples become wrinkles, life would be more peaceful and secure. Yet, I'm starting the New Year and I'm scared to death.

Ruthy

The prince feels as though she's twisting a knife in his belly. They've tried not to talk about it until now, not to say it. And now it's here, out on the table between them, the fact that he, who had promised her a palace and a fairy tale, who promised her the life of a princess, and happily ever after, hasn't kept his promise. He failed to pave her life with indulgences; he failed to provide her with a life of real luxury, not to mention living without a care, just like they once dreamed, like she once dreamed and like she deserved. And he feels pathetic. And it burns his heart, that sentence of hers, that the money she'll earn will help them.

He wants to shout that she doesn't know how hard it is out there, and how hard he tries, and he deserves a kind word for nevertheless succeeding. Because, after all, he provides for them adequately, even if he isn't a hotshot provider like her girlfriends' husbands or a bunch of the guys he grew up with. He drives to work every morning in his little white company car, and looks up at those women in the huge, shiny jeeps stuck in traffic with him. And this sour sense of failure – that he's not good enough, not man enough – chokes him and he says that if it's for the money, then she doesn't have to. He'll probably get another promotion soon.

And she says that she wants to.

"And it won't be too difficult for you?" he asks.

"So…it will be a bit difficult," she says.

"Okay," he says. "It's your decision."

And there's a silence. She waits for him to say that he'll help. He doesn't say it. And she understands. She understands that not only has he left her the decision, he's also left her the responsibility. Just as they promised each other that they wouldn't. Once upon a time, when they decided about things together, when they had a shared goal. Now they are two people standing on different sides of the barricade, each of them trying to shove the border just a few more inches into the other's territory, to gain a little more maneuvering space for himself or herself, to shed the responsibility, get some relief. And it angers her. She wants to remind him that she isn't doing this only for herself. But she doesn't.

And he tells her to do it if this is what she wants.

And this is how the priority of her work is defined in their lives.

The princess doesn't go out to work because she has to. They can live without the money she'll earn. Frugally, as they've lived up until now. She's going to work for herself. Because she wants to. It's her decision. For herself. She hadn't realized that these words – that she doesn't have to, she *wants* to – would place her work second in its importance. Or maybe third, after his work and the children.

# 17

*And [she] said, If it please the king...*

(Esther 8:5)

My girlfriend invited us to her son's birthday. "It'll be fun," she said. "We've invited all the children from the preschool, and some friends of mine you've already met." I hated these events. Events with children and a lot of people I didn't know. But I didn't want to bail out because I wanted to do the right thing. For my girlfriend, to whom it was important; for my son, who would probably have fun; and for my daughter, who also loved these events. Or at least, that's what I told myself. And I went. I cursed myself the minute I walked into the room. I tried to ignore the stares the other mothers gave my daughter, the misunderstandings, the whispers – and the brave ones, those who asked interested questions, who forced me to explain, smile, play it down. I also tried to ignore the other children, their sweetness, the ease with which they conducted themselves, asking for potato chips, cooperating, playing with the surprises and knowing well enough not to eat clay.

"She's eating the clay!" one of the mothers shouted and swooped down on her, on my daughter, with two others, trying to extract the tiny morsel out of her mouth. "Leave her alone!" I shouted. "Don't touch her!" An uncomfortable silence descended. I didn't tell them what other strange things she eats.

I apologized to my friend, and asked her to let me off the hook in the future. And from then on I avoided going to these events. Joint afternoons with other children weren't good for me. Neither were the apologies for the mess my daughter left after her. I think both sides were relieved.

Slowly, most of my friends had become mothers. Each of them was immersed in her own world and in her diapers, and the relationships dissolved. With this particular friend, and with several others that I can count on one hand, I kept in touch, but only in the evenings. Even though we were few, it still required endless exhausting coordination. This one doesn't have a babysitter. This one's son is sick. This one has to go with her husband to some event. And this one has a ton of work.

Usually, we'd meet at one of our houses, and once in a long while, on festive occasions, we managed to find a stolen evening, dress up in our best clothes, and go out to a bar to have a drink. Four women who were destined for greatness in their youth; four women who could move mountains if they just wanted to: four mothers. And we'd sit and talk. This one talked about problems at work, this one about confrontations with the boss, this one about childrearing problems, all of us about problems with teachers and nannies, and about the husband who didn't understand, or wasn't sensitive enough, or romantic enough. This is what we met for. This was what we needed. To share with each other the tiny details that no one else had the energy or strength to follow, or to examine; to go on and on about the little encumbrances that bothered and worried us, and in exchange give each other a shoulder to lean on. We met in order to get a load off our chests. So that someone would listen to the difficulties and problems, listen to that awful thing that happened to us, or what our mother told us, and how dare she, and to confirm that even though we're miserable, we're surviving, and coping, and we're so brave.

And I knew that they got together with other mothers in the afternoons, with their children. Because that's what other mothers of little children are supposed to do.

> Maybe I'm laughing from fear, because of something that just happened at our place. I told my husband that I want to invite my oldest son's friends because he seems a bit lonely. This, of course, involves entertaining children who are part of Attila the Hun's group, which means parting with several precious articles in the house. But I'll do anything to get a smile on the lips of my sweet boy. My husband stared at me with disbelief and asked, "Where are you getting this from? Can't you see that the boy is happy and content? What party? What do you mean, 'lonely'?!"
>
> "I don't know," I stammered, and searched for an answer for myself.
>
> Now I understand why I don't earn more. Because instead of investing all my hours in paid work, I spend them, with so much love, joy, and cheerfulness, clucking around my children's desires. Oh, now I get it. Thanks for the enlightenment, Buddha.
>
> Talia

The princess starts looking for work. She sits down and goes over the ads in the newspaper and on the Internet. Among all the ads and job offers, she crosses out the fields of industry and manufacture, engineering and technology, security and cleaning.

She's looking for something in the humanities. That's what she loves and that's what she studied. She examines the small print that appears under education, instruction and caretakers; marketing and sales; fashion, textile and beauty.

Energetic and responsible person needed to market cakes: base + percentage + car. Full-time job. She's energetic, she's the champion of cakes, but a full-time job is out of the question. And it also doesn't have the same area code as the palace.

A garage needs an experienced secretary, computer-oriented, with a desire to succeed. Full-time job. She isn't really all that good with computers. She has the desire to succeed, but how successful can she be as a garage secretary? And it doesn't really open any options for the future.

And experience. Everyone wants experience and she isn't experienced. Import company needs field agent. Experience mandatory. Full-time job. Fashion chain needs district manager. Experience in leading fashion chains, fax CV. Well, she does have the desire. Secretary/student for law firm, afternoons, Word proficient. Full-time. Full-time for afternoons? That means all night. No wonder they're looking for a student.

Agent, sales-oriented, credibility, highly industrious, independent, must own a car, 30+. That looks pretty good. She writes down the phone number and thinks of all the things she once dreamed of doing. She dreamed of becoming an art teacher. She even has a degree, but she doesn't have a teaching diploma. She dreamed of running her own business, but for that one needs a financial investment, and it's too scary, and who would invest in her anyway? She doesn't dare think of asking the bank for a loan. A loan for what purpose? What would she say? She has no idea what she knows how to do. Design. She has great taste. She could have been great at interior decorating, but she'd have to study for that. Besides, she's already studied; she won't go now and study for four years, and then work another two or three years in an architect's office from morning till night. That's for young women. And she's not at an age for new beginnings. She's a thirty-three-year-old princess, and she has a useless degree that's gathering dust somewhere and doesn't interest anyone. And she has no experience. And nobody wrote in their ad that they're looking for a princess. No one needs princesses nowadays.

My name is Tamara. We corresponded once on the subject of work. I asked for advice and you gave me emotional support. It was good. And lo and behold - once again I've returned to the circle of job-seekers. I accept it being a long and draining procedure, but what makes it really difficult is the procedure itself.

A company advertises an open position through a manpower service. Tamara makes the effort of sending her resume and a relevant letter. The HR manager makes contact and conducts a phone interview, during which she questions me about my positive and negative traits and summons me to the evaluation center. The big day arrives. Tamara wears her best clothes, pays her hard-earned money to the nearest parking lot attendant, and enlists her most upbeat energies for this wonderful day.

Now the big moment arrives: group dynamics. A group of adults with employment experience constructing paper airplanes, preparing presentations, and conducting negotiations over

the paper planes. It isn't enough that I have to
market and represent myself every time anew. When
will they understand that adults, not children,
are standing behind these resumes?

Hey, if you hear about a job opening in
marketing/public relations, etc., I'll be more
than happy to show you how I build paper planes.

Tamara

There was only one thing that inspired me more than writing and
made me happy. One big ray of sunshine that during all those
darkest, gloomy moments illuminated my soul. My oldest child.
My sweet boy with his big blue eyes, and his thumb in his mouth,
who from the age of two and a half accepted the fact that his sister
could tear up any one of his drawings, break any one of his toys,
and wake him up at night. Who knew that he had to be considerate
toward her, that we had to watch out so that she wouldn't get lost,
who knew that the entire world revolved around his sister, who
doesn't speak and doesn't answer. He lived with all these people
walking around his house, and he never complained. And he was
never mad at her. He never hit her, pushed her, or yelled at her. He
was the best little boy in the world. Only in the morning, when
he had to go to preschool, he would cry terribly. Cry and ask why
he had to go to school, why he couldn't be like his sister. And stay
at home.

# 18

*Who can find a virtuous woman?*

(Proverbs 31:10)

The princess, who runs from one job interview to another, starts realizing that it won't be easy finding a job in which she can pick up the heirs from preschool at one o'clock. She, who up until now was part of a small group of mothers who reported every day at midday to pick up their children, the proud group, the wonderful group that doesn't joyfully throw their children into the preschool for eight hours, knows that she'll have to give up her exclusive membership in this lovely association: the Association of Dedicated Mothers. Those mothers, who arrive first and converse briefly with the teacher, and then leave the preschool while glancing pityingly at the children who have to stay until four o'clock; those mothers who prepare a nutritious lunch every day, sit down with their children and patiently listen to what happened to them, involved in their lives and in the community.

And she is a woman who up to the present moment has believed in what she is doing, in the fact that she's giving everything she has to her children, that her sacrifice is the highest level of love and motherly dedication. Now she discovers that in order to go out to work, she'll have to shove aside everything that she has considered holy until now. She'll have to switch sides and become part of the group of mothers whom she didn't understand until now: the group scorned by herself and her friends in their exclusive and amazing group. Because she'll either have to leave them at the preschool for several more hours or find a nanny. And not for her dream job. Not so she can become a brain surgeon, or a tower-constructing architect, or a high-income manager in a high-tech company. She'll be doing it for a pretty dreary job, in a pretty dreary office, that maybe, one day, in several years' time, will lead her to something that comes close to being interesting. And she decides to leave the heirs in the preschool, and swears that she'll do her job quickly and efficiently, and pick them up way before four o'clock. That way, they'll only have to stay another hour, two hours max. It won't be so bad.

> I have a daughter in preschool and a son in first grade. Three times a week he finishes school at 1:40 and she finishes at 1:20. Paying for two after-school activity day care centers eats up my entire salary to the last penny. This is a problem that can be resolved when a mother works part-time. Then, she can help with homework, and experience preschool and school with her children. Unfortunately, it's very hard to find part-time jobs. I can't look for a job that exceeds the 8:00-1:00 hours, and it also has to be close to home, otherwise the nanny will earn more than I do during the extra hours that I've added to the job.
>
> Adina

I knew that I wouldn't succeed if writing continued being a hobby. I realized that if I really wanted my story to become a real book,

I'd have to give it everything I had – really submerge myself in it, with all my soul, with all my heart. And I didn't have time, and I wasn't even sure if I had any place left in my soul.

I was an angry and bitter woman, sad and desperate, who had become addicted to struggling against demons and dragons on a twenty-four-hour basis. To make time for writing, I had to search my soul and find the resolve to change the priorities of the entire household, of the entire family, and I was scared. Would my family have to pay a high price for no more than a hopeless and desperate attempt at trying to make a crazy dream come true? I was afraid of what would happen to my little girl if I wasn't there to give her my heart and soul, what would happen to my oldest child, what would happen to this family, for whose survival and function my man struggled with all his might. This was a war in which I dug the trenches and manned the line, but I didn't give it even one moment of hope or contentment. I dragged all of us down with it, and forced everyone to be sad and hurt. And I knew that for several hours a day, I'd have to pull myself out of it, out of there. And for the first time in a long time, I realized that if I didn't have a dream, if I didn't have something of my own, I'd destroy what we *did* have. And I decided that I wasn't giving up, that I was fighting for my book.

After two years during which my little girl was home-schooled, and I insisted on supervising her every second, every minute – during which I heard every peep she made and was proud of my dedication – I dared suggest the idea that we send her to a preschool for children like herself for half a day. I told myself that it was for her own good, and that she'd get what she needed there, and that they're experienced and know what they're doing. And my man also said that he thought the time had come, and that it was the right thing to do. And I didn't know if I should believe him – or myself. I didn't know if he was saying that because he thought I couldn't handle it anymore. And after all, maybe that's what I was saying myself. And I felt as though I was sending her to preschool just so I'd have several hours in the morning – that I was sending her there just because I was weak, because I dared think of myself – and I was ashamed.

She started going to preschool. At night I was awake with her, in the morning I worked, and at noon I was with her again; in the afternoon I ran around with both of them from one after-school activity to the other, enrichment activities, occupational clinics, speech therapy clinics, the doctor, and errands, and I was exhausted and bleary-eyed, but I didn't allow myself to miss one minute with her. And even though I hired a nanny to come and help me out, I still couldn't manage. And I felt spoiled for not managing. For not being able to go out alone with both of them without something happening. Because all it took was for me to turn my head and let go of my little girl's hand and she'd immediately get lost. In the shopping center, in the mall, in the supermarket, everywhere, she could just disappear. And there was no point in calling out for her, because she didn't respond. It happened to me again and again. When I took out my purse just for a second to pay for ice cream, or when my son asked me to unwrap something for him, that was it. And if there was a road, then I'd immediately run to check that there wasn't a little girl who had been hit by a car. And my oldest, only a little boy himself, was already experienced and knew how to warn me, "Mommy, she's going," and knew how to run after her, and hold her, and help me search for her. Search without yelling her name. Quietly we'd search.

These moments when she was lost and my heart would beat erratically scarred me with the notion that I wasn't good enough or responsible enough. And then there were the stares of those people, who stood around a sweet, smiling four-year-old child, trying to ask her name, and asking her where her mommy was, and when I came, they looked at me as if I was a failure. A mother who loses her child. And I felt like a failure, even though holding her was like holding quicksilver. My son was already five and a half years old, and whenever he was with me, she was there too, and she was the center of attention, and the only places we could go to were places where we could take her as well, where there weren't many people, and there weren't any roads, and she couldn't get lost. And that's how we'd wander around in the afternoons, together. A mother, two children, and a nanny. Because the mother couldn't handle both of them alone. A mother who doesn't work, and doesn't earn, and employs a nanny. And still can't cope.

▪ ▪ ▪

The princess finds a job. Part-time as a secretary in a real-estate agency. She takes the job because she knows that she'll be able to make progress from there. She has a tidy plan. She'll work there for several months, learn the business, because she's a fast learner, and then take a course, and become a realtor herself. All she needs is to sell one apartment a month. What's the problem to sell one apartment a month, with her outgoing, personal charm? Who can resist her? And that will be enough to change everything. Maybe she'll even open her own agency. They'll go on vacations, go out to restaurants and order without looking at the prices on the menu, and one day, perhaps they'll even replace the derelict palace and move to a larger apartment. Which she'll find at a steal. Within a year or two, she believes, she'll already strike out on her own. And she starts working.

On her first day she wakes up way before the alarm clock and gets dressed, having prepared her clothes the day before. She brings her children to preschool, the teacher compliments her on her appearance, everyone wishes her luck, and then she goes over to kiss the heiress, and reminds her that she's staying today at the afternoon day care center, just to eat lunch with all the children, and then Mommy will come to take her home. The heiress bursts into heart-wrenching tears. "No!" she screams, "I want to do what we always do, I want you, I don't want the yucky food here, I want to go home. I want to go home now!" And the princess strokes the heiress, and promises her that everything will be just fine, and that the food is delicious. And the heiress says that she was the one who said that the food is disgusting, and the princess promises her that she'll come as fast as she can, and she looks at the clock and knows that if she doesn't leave now she'll be late, and the preschool teacher sees her glancing at the clock and tells her, "Go, it'll be fine, in a minute she'll forget all about it." And she walks backwards, trying not to turn her back on the heiress, blowing her kisses while the preschool teacher holds her with all her might so she won't run after her, and the heiress cries like she's never cried before because the princess has always stayed with her until she agreed to let Mommy go and shouts after her, "Mommy, Mommy!"

The princess, who had applied her makeup so beautifully, looks in the little mirror in the car and sees how her tears have smudged all her efforts. She repairs some of the damage and goes to the office for her very first day, and her main occupation all day is to ignore the lump in her throat and make an effort not to glance at the clock every minute. But she does look at it every minute, and time stands still. Half an hour, and another hour, and she feels that the pain of the abandoned heiress is racking her entire body. She curses herself for causing her such pain – who knows what scars this day inflicted upon her – and she barely hears what everyone is telling her, what they're trying to teach her. And the minute the clock strikes one, she smiles at her boss, hitches her bag on her shoulder, and says thank you. And he also looks at his watch, and she smiles apologetically, aware that she's making a mistake, and that she should stay until he tells her to go. But her heart is in shreds of agony because of the heiress's misery – she's probably been crying for hours – and she says that she'll see him tomorrow and leaves the office. And she runs to the car.

> When I was a child, I was once walking with my neighbor down the street. On the way, she approached a woman I knew who ran an appliance repair shop on the street where I grew up. I have no idea what the neighbor said to her, but I'll never forget what that woman answered my neighbor. "She's a street child." Yes, that's what she said about me, because I'd wander around with a key hanging around my neck because my mother was at work. But I think that this is the reality that shaped my life and I'm grateful for every minute of it. Because this sentence generated a lot of thought in my adult life, as well as my enormous capacity to give.
>
> Libby

I began realizing that I'd been so concerned about my little girl that I hadn't spent time with the others. I hadn't sat quietly with my stepson, just me and him, for such a long time, and once we used to do this a lot, and we were so close, and I knew that I didn't want to lose this relationship, and that I had to carve out a place for it. And it hurt me that I hadn't seen it before, that I hadn't understood it before, and I was angry with myself. And I realized that I didn't spend time alone with my son at all, and that I should spend more time with him, just me and him. He needed me, my oldest child, who was really so young. And he needed not to always be around his sister, and not to be with me only when I was concentrating on her. He needed time during which he didn't have to be considerate and helpful and shoved aside. I was angry with myself because he was such a good boy, so accommodating. And I was tormented. I decided that twice a week I'd spend time with him only. And twice a week, when I was with him, I sent the nanny to the pool with my little girl.

My little girl had always loved water. I hate pools, yet my little girl loved them. During the first years, the pool was a place where I could be with her, hug her, touch her, and feel that we were together. And I taught her how to swim. At the age of two and a half, she already knew how to swim. That's why, when I realized that my oldest needed some time alone with me, I decided that the best thing to do was to send my little girl to the pool with the nanny. She couldn't get lost there either. After several months of this arrangement, one day I brought her to the pool myself. Suddenly, I felt the stares. The life guard, the swimming teacher, the other mothers, even the guy from the refreshment stand all stared at me. I felt their glances like knives in my back. *Here's that mother*, the knives twisted, *who sends her daughter only with the nanny, who doesn't really care about her child.* And I wanted to yell at them that they don't see me during the other days – and there were so many other days – when I was only with her, when I took her wherever she felt like going, and turned off my cell phone, and sang all the words to her children's songs at the top of my lungs, clapping hands with her enthusiastically.

*I'm an amazing mother*, I wanted to tell all those stares. *I just can't stand swimming pools; I can't stand walking around in a bathing suit, even if my little girl really loves to, and I did it for so long, and the fact that I stopped doing it doesn't mean that I'm a neglectful mother. And anyway, my son needs me. Needs me a bit for himself.* And their stares hurt me, so I decided to come more frequently with my child to the pool. So that everyone would know how dedicated I am. How wonderful. I reported at the pool a week later. And I sat outside the pool for an hour, looking at her. And I felt like an idiot. I felt as though I had wasted an hour on something superfluous. An hour during which I could have spent time with my son, who needed me so much. And instead, I made an appearance. And I sat there and got mad at them. For making me play this game. This stupid game that we had going between us. Between one mother and another. An international competition of sacrifice and investment. A competition in which the dedicated mothers stood on one side, and the working mothers who juggled between work and family stood on the other side.

And this competition sizzled and raged, and the dedicated mothers were condescending toward the working mothers, who in turn, were condescending toward the dedicated mothers for choosing to raise children and not to work, and said that they spent their entire day in cafes. It was a struggle of justification, because each side justified itself by condescending to the other side, who had chosen differently. It was a war that left the women on both sides with the feeling that they're not good enough.

A war in which everyone was left bruised and bleeding and feeling like a failure. Feeling as though they'd sacrificed. And I didn't understand how I hadn't seen that those women I once thought were my friends, my partners – my support group – were actually a judging team. They supported only those who had chosen as they did, but judged and criticized all the others and thought they were better than them. And I was angry that I even cared about this game of appearances, the stupid, dizzying game of *what will everyone say*, only so other mothers, neighbors, grandmothers, teachers, counselors, and random women won't think that I'm a bad mother.

And no one, not for a minute, would have thought that my husband was a bad father because he didn't sit at the pool twice a week and waste an hour watching his daughter swim. And I kept silent. I choked, but I kept silent.

Why is it that we, the women, are the ones who always have to go to seminars? Why are we the ones who complain? Why do I have a feeling that men don't understand us? Why is everything so simple and clear for men? Grrr!

Batya

# 19

*As cold waters to a thirsty soul...*

(Proverbs 25:25)

The princess arrives to pick up the heiress from preschool and
finds her napping on one of the small, thin mattresses in a row
with all the other children of the working mothers. The row that
she was so proud that her children weren't part of. The princess
asks the teacher, fearfully, how the heiress held up, and the
teacher tells her that she stopped crying several minutes after she
left and that she was really fine. Like always. The princess doesn't
know whether she should be glad or sad, and says that she was so
worried, and the teacher says that she doesn't understand why she
was worried. And the princess takes the heiress and goes to pick
up the heir from kindergarten.

After a while, the heirs grow used to eating lunch at school, and
gradually, the princess starts learning the work and befriending
the realtors. Everyone appreciates her and counts on her and
consults with her, and sometimes they even call during the
afternoon to ask something, and she always answers gladly, and
she goes out of her way and manages to get through the summer
in one piece, paying her entire salary to summer camps, and in
addition has to ask for help with the heirs from the queen and
her mother, even though she hates asking for help – not only

from them, but in general – but she swallows her pride. And the moment comes when summer ends, and the heir starts first grade. And when she sees him with his large schoolbag, she can't help but cry. The prince is also very excited.

And she knows that the time has come.

The princess asks for a meeting with the office manager, and tells him that she wants to start a course and earn a certificate and start working as a realtor. He tells her that he thinks she'll be great and asks her not to leave the office. "We can't manage without you," he says, and she's so proud. She says that it never even crossed her mind to leave, that it's only twice a week. She'll manage. She leaves the meeting, and she's so happy, and she tells all the other realtors that she's starting the course, and she's surprised that not everyone is as happy for her, and one of them even says that it's not for her. That she's too nice for the job. She's slightly insulted, and then she realizes that he fears for his job. That he's afraid she'll take his job away from him. He's afraid of her. And she'll no longer receive all the support that she has received until now as the beloved secretary. Now, she's a competitor. She's in the race. It scares her but she knows that she's good, and that she can do it, and apparently, so do they, otherwise they wouldn't be afraid. And twice a week she leaves the children in school until four o'clock and participates in the course.

■ ■ ■

I continued writing during every spare minute, and I went to another publishing house.

But this time, I prepared myself differently. I lowered my expectations. I tried not to even hope that they'd like it, even though deep inside I dreamed that they'd faint, and I told them that I was ready to hear everything, every comment, to write and rewrite, but I just didn't want to hear no. I asked them to please notice that there was something there. To try to see, in the forest of words, that there was a good story there. And they did notice. They said that it wasn't bad, that it was actually pretty good, but that it needed work – a lot of work. And as painful as that was, the feeling was different. It was different because I knew that this wasn't an abstract dream, but something that could really happen, because someone believed in me, and someone was with me, guiding me, and I started feeling as if it could really happen. My dream could come true one day. And this publishing house signed a contract with me. I received an advance payment. I made money after years that I hadn't. I was on the right track. It wasn't just a dream after all. I was right – I wasn't just amusing myself – there was a good reason for which I had painstakingly collected all these fragmented hours, for which I had fought and worked so hard. And for the next six months, I continued writing.

> Lately, I have a growing suspicion that I've been cheated all the way. Cheated by how I've been educated, by how I've been led to believe all those theories that you've described. I'm not like that. It's not nice to push. I should wait until someone sees how talented I am. I should be gentle, kind, modest. You described everything so beautifully and with such accuracy and pain. The truth is that I was slightly surprised because you look too young to have grown up in the same atmosphere in which I was raised. Anyway, you look very young. I hope the younger generation

has more brains, and that the young women are
different from my generation.
Aviva

One day, as the princess is driving back from the course, she gets stuck in a traffic jam. She looks at her watch and knows that there's no chance that she'll arrive in time to pick up the children. And she's angry with herself for staying that extra minute. She shouldn't have. But she thought it was important just for once to stay back with the other students in the course, who always go together to drink coffee, chat, and compare agencies. She knows it's important to make contacts, and not always grab her bag and rush out of the classroom, because as it is, she's something of an eccentric, slightly older than everyone, always in a bit more of a rush than everyone else, and she knows that it's important that she sometimes stay a bit longer and make friends. But now she's alone in the car, stuck in this infuriating traffic jam that won't budge an inch, and time isn't standing still.

3:52. No chance that she'll make it. And she can already imagine her heirs waiting for her with big eyes overflowing with sadness – children whose mother didn't come to pick them up. The only ones whose mother forgot them.

3:57. *She doesn't love me*, they're probably telling themselves, *she doesn't care about me, I'm not important to her*, and guilt racks her, etching scars in her heart, which are now also carved in the little souls of her young heirs, scratched and bruised for all eternity, teeming with fear of abandonment, irreversibly scarred. And she phones another mother, asking her to take her little girl. She's already left but she'll go back for her if that's what she wants. "No, no big deal," she says. And she calls another mother, who says that she's already in the park and that they should join them later on.

3:59. Now she'll get those glares, from the heiress's assistant teacher, and the woman in charge of the after-school activity club in the heir's school. Those glares that say, wordlessly, what they think about mothers like herself. Confused mothers, who forget life's priorities, that children come before careers, and she feels so selfish and wants to say that she's trying, that she's well aware of priorities, but sometimes things go wrong, sometimes things happen, and not because she doesn't care, but because of the fucking traffic jam, and she feels as though she's about to faint.

4:00. She calls the woman in charge of the after-school activity club. "I'll be there in a couple of minutes." And a call beeps in from the heiress's preschool. "I'm on my way." And one more traffic light.

4:03. She wants to scream and cry, and she remembers that look she got at work when she went out to her course, and the looks that she got at the course when she left while everyone was still standing around chatting, the young women and men, who can come home in the evening, which she can no longer afford to do, and she thinks how much more of an effort she'll have to invest in order to work. She knows that there are people who have time to see apartments only during the evenings, and there are those who will want to view an apartment at five o' clock in the afternoon, and she doesn't know how she'll manage, because her children are still small, and as it is, real estate agents fight over every deal, and if she doesn't give everything she has then she won't make it, and maybe he was right, maybe she doesn't have what it takes. Because she sees them, those other realtors, most of them men. They're always available and can always meet everyone's requests. They aren't time limited; they answer their phones like junkies. There's this one woman realtor who's just like them, who works around the clock. But she knows that she isn't like her, that she knows her priorities, that the heirs' young souls are more important, and she realizes that as much as she tries during the day to be as efficient as possible, and just as wonderful, and to achieve as much as she can in minimum time, she'll never be able to keep up with them. With those people who give everything they've got. Because occasionally, she's going to get a phone call notifying her that her son isn't feeling well, and she'll have to go pick him up, and she'll let someone else take care of the client, and it won't be her sale. And she presses on the horn, knowing that it's futile, that it won't help move the traffic jam, and if only she could stop time, stop the clock. Stop it. Freeze it.

4:04. So it will just stand still for a moment and let her catch up. But the clock doesn't stop. And no one stops, and she starts realizing that no one even sees it. No one knows how hard she's trying. And now her heir is crying. And everyone can see how she's screwing up. And she feels dizzy. She feels as though she's on a merry-go-round ride and she can't get off in the middle, and it's stirring everything within her and causing her a bitter, oppressive nausea of failure. And she feels so alone. She feels as though her shoulders are too narrow to carry this burden, to carry this responsibility all by herself, and she knows that no one is truly aware of what she's doing, of what she's going through, and the price she's paying for trying to do everything. And she remembers that lovely evening, at their wedding, when she spun around with her white ball gown, with her hair that had been tended to for hours, and her makeup, floating on clouds, expecting happily ever after, and how she felt as though she were a real princess.

And she furiously presses the horn again and thinks how easy it is for the prince. How much quiet he has when he goes to work; he just goes. And how easy it is for him to work. He doesn't have to worry who'll take the kids, who'll pick them up, what they need, what they ate, why they cried, what has to be bought, and more than anything, he doesn't ask himself if it's okay that he went. Because the prince will always have her, and she's the one taking care of the children. They're her responsibility. And she can't understand how this has happened to her, to them. How did they turn into one of those couples that they swore not to turn into? Those couples where the woman takes care of the children, and the husband goes to work. And she knows that if she continues working, it won't be the last time she's late to pick them up.

4:05. And she can't breathe.

> I'm married and a mother to a first-grader and a two-year-old, and I work full-time as a manager in a company. I cope, like everyone else, with the imbalance of being a working mother. Every night, I go to bed and pray that tomorrow, everything will be different, and I'll succeed in what I want. I want to get up at 6:00 when the alarm clock rings, and not stay in bed because I'm too tired to move. I want to be patient in the morning without nagging, "Come on, already, wash your face, eat, we have to go." I want to pick up my youngest from preschool (which doesn't always happen) and get home by 5:00 at the latest. I want to take them to a playground once a week, to friends once a week, to have friends over once a week, and once a week just to sit with them at home and play (without the television blaring in

the background, and the laundry, and the dishes).
I want to prepare a healthy dinner (not frozen
pizza or microwave meals). To stop giving them
too many snacks and candies. I want to come home
and bake fancy cookies and bring them to the
office. I want to sit a bit more with my oldest
on his homework, take him to his after-school
activities and not only bring him back from them.
I want to exercise twice a week and not only run
up and down the office stairs. I want to get up
early on Saturday, drink coffee, travel, and not
only think when I'll find the time to sleep. I want
to sit with my husband in the evening, cuddle
with him, talk, and not fall asleep on the sofa
exhausted. I want to go on a weekend retreat,
without the children, recharge my batteries
and energies. I want a little more money in my
bank account; it would help me breathe easier. I
want to get together with Sharon, and Reva, and
Hadar, whom I haven't seen in a long time. I want
quality time with my father and my mother. I want
to smile at the children, and not get upset at
what they're doing, because all in all, they're
lovely, and I'm the one who's exhausted, angry,
impatient, and waiting for them to go to sleep so
I'll have some peace and quiet for myself. But
my youngest won't fall asleep if I'm not sitting
next to him. I want to do a boot camp week to
teach him how to fall asleep by himself, during
which he'll cry bitter tears. And yet, I derive
so much strength from how he cuddles into me,
kisses me on the mouth and cheek, and the special
way he has of saying, "Mommy, I love you." I want

```
to pursue my dream of making a sister for my
boys. Mostly, I want.
```
```
Karen
```

I finished the book and it was just about to be published. Even though I knew that I shouldn't expect too much, because so many books are published every year, and so many of them disappear, swallowed up or forgotten, I couldn't help dreaming that it would become a runaway success, and that many people would read it and respond, and listen. And my life would change and at least in one thing I'd once again become successful and I'd know that I did it, that I won, I arrived, and that I have a place of honor and significance. I believed that there was something in this book, and if only it succeeded, I thought, it would grant me my desired place in the world. I'd be somebody. And one day, I opened the door to my house, and a box was waiting there for me. Inside were twenty copies of my book, containing four years of struggle, of accumulated minutes and moments, disappointments and hope; and I stroked the cover.

That evening we were invited to friends. I brought them a copy of the book. There were all sorts of people there, and everyone congratulated me, and I felt on top of the world.

Someone I didn't know read what was written on the back of the book. "Isn't it intriguing?" I asked.

"No," she told me. I must have looked pretty surprised, because then she said, "Sorry, but I always say the truth."

# 20

*Why weepest thou? and why eatest thou not?*
*and why is thy heart grieved?*

(1 Samuel 1:8)

The prince comes home one day, this time pretty early and in a good mood, because he found out that he got the promotion he's been waiting on for so long. When he enters, the princess is just giving the heirs their bath, washing the conditioner from the heiress's head, and when she hears him put down his briefcase, she immediately yells out to him, "You're here at last, come and take them out," and she dries her hands, and when she leaves to make room for him, she reminds him to wipe them down thoroughly because the heir has a bit of a cold, and the heiress likes now only the pink pajamas, and if he's already at it, maybe he can read them a story, she says to him, and adds that she's going to the living room, that she needs a moment of peace, because she had a terrible day, and he can't imagine the traffic jam she got stuck in, and she starts telling him about that horrible traffic jam, and how she was late for their poor children, and she wants to talk to him about something because things are really hard for her, and she thought about it and she wants him to arrange one day a week when he'll be the one to pick them up at four, and he says that he can't and it's actually related to something good that he wants to tell her, and she asks him about what, and he says that they'll talk later, and she says tell me now, and he tells her that he got the promotion, and she asks why he didn't call her sooner, and he says that he didn't want to tell her on the phone, and the heiress starts crying that she wants to get out, and that she needs to wipe her eyes because she's got soap in them, and it burns, and she cries terribly, and the princess says to him that she doesn't understand how he didn't want to tell her the news immediately, and the heir wants to get out too, and the princess tells the prince that they'll talk about it later, and the heir climbs out and drips water on the floor, and the princess tells the prince to look how the boy is dripping water all over the house, and she's so tired already, and the prince tells her that she doesn't have to work so hard, and now he'll definitely get a raise, and she turns to him and tells him that it would be foolish of her to give up on it now, and she also raises her voice a bit, because in just a short while she'll get her certificate, and she'll earn a fine salary, and she wipes down the heir, and besides, it's not only because of the money, she says, it's the fact that the children barely see him, and he isn't involved enough in their lives, and she asks if he's going to be working longer hours, and he says, and his voice is also approaching a shout, that his father also worked like this and he doesn't remember his father ever picking him up from school, and it didn't make him feel as though his father had neglected him because his father provided for them, and he's also providing for them, and she tells him quietly, not in front of the children, we'll talk later, and she goes to the living room and collapses, because she still hasn't pulled herself together from that traffic jam, and for the first time that day she sits in peace.

And she thinks about the fact that it wasn't even important enough for him to call her and announce his promotion. And she thinks about how she needed someone to give her a kind word when she was stuck in the traffic jam, and she didn't call him either. And she understands that he's no longer really her friend. Not like he promised to be. And she's not really his friend. They only have shared children, and a joint address on which they haven't even finished paying half of the mortgage.

Your man is interested in soccer, but he'll never notice if the children don't have a winter coat, or if last year's shoes are already small. That may be true about men like my father, who is 78, may he live a long life, but things have changed since then. I know that my situation doesn't represent everyone - I am singlehandedly raising my teenage son and daughter, and yes, this week I went with them to shop for winter clothes, without any woman sending me to do so, because there isn't a woman in the vicinity to take care of them (or of me).

I work hard, get home in the evening, and then my daughter announces that tomorrow she has an algebra test and that I have to help her study, and my son has an English assignment, and dinner has to be made, and they fight a little, and to make a long story short, when I finally sit down (collapse or dive into semi-consciousness would be more accurate) at 11:00 in front of the television, I don't even see what's running on the screen. I just enjoy the quiet for a bit.

I was a good husband. I loved my wife. I enjoyed spending time with her, talking with her at the end of the day, seeing a good movie with

her, and we laughed a lot. In the end, she left me
and the children and went off with someone who's
the exact opposite. A bad character who makes his
woman miserable (in short, the bad boy). But try
figuring out women and what they're looking for.

Danny

The prince takes the heirs to their rooms, dresses them in their
pajamas, tells them a story, pulls the covers over them, and kisses
them. And then he stays with them some more. Enjoying their
sweet scent of pure cleanliness and listening to them breathing.
And he doesn't even feel like leaving their room, leaving the quiet
and the warmth. He isn't up to the conversation that will start
now with the princess, an inevitable conversation whose end he
already knows. And he doesn't understand how it happened that
instead of celebrating his promotion, they managed to have a
fight. He desperately wanted to celebrate with her; he wanted her
to be happy for them, for both of them. And he wanted her to
be happy for him, because she knew how hard it was for him to
achieve this, and how he waited for it, and he couldn't believe how
he even thought, all the way home, about the way she'd look at
him when he'd tell her about the promotion. He couldn't believe
that he hoped she'd have that look he hasn't seen in so long, that
look she used to give him.

And he realizes that he's waiting for morning. He's looking
forward to going to work. Because with all the difficulty and the
challenges there, there's also laughter and action, and camaraderie,
and people who appreciate him. And especially her, the new
girl, who smiles at him every morning, and laughs brightly and
heartily at every one of his jokes, and he realizes that that's what

he's waiting for more than anything. Her looks and her smiles. He knows that they're flirting. And he knows that it isn't a good idea but she's the one who started it. She's the one who brought a cake one morning and sent him slightly vulgar e-mails; she's the one who told him about the dreamy massage that a masseur gave her and recommended that he get one as well; she's the one who told him on her birthday that she doesn't want him to bring her anything but himself and he's well aware that he likes it. He hasn't felt like this for a long time, and he feels so good; it feels so pleasant to him. Much more pleasant than coming home and fighting again with his frazzled and unsatisfied princess who finds hardship in every day.

# 21

*Things too wonderful for me, which I knew not.*

(Job 42:3)

My book succeeded far beyond expectations. It succeeded even
more than I had dared dream. It was a best seller. After two years
of unsuccessful pregnancies, seven years of motherhood, four
years of raising a special child, which together constituted almost
a decade of giving, investing, rescuing, caretaking, wars, survival
struggles, keeping promises made to others, and trying along the
way to keep some of those promises made to myself; after four
years of writing born of a desperate struggle for every second of
free time during which I ran to the computer, of the attempt to
also be a wonderful mother, a lovely daughter, a wife, and a friend,
while stumbling and failing in every one of these things, scratched
and bruised from feelings of guilt, agonized but reminding myself
that there was a large and important goal, and that if I succeeded
then one day I'd reach that place of accomplishment and peace
and joy that I yearned for so desperately, I had done it. I had
reached the moment when I was supposed to dance on the top
of the world, celebrate my success and the fact that I was earning
money once again, that I had done something real, that I had
made it. That was the moment in which I was supposed to touch
happiness. And my man hugged me and told me how wonderful I

was, and I went out for a drink with the girls, and my mother was proud, and the check was deposited in the bank account, and that was it. That was just about it.

I had waited for this moment for so long, and now it was here, and everything stayed just the same. I was an adult woman, exhausted, angry, with a sour face, the corners of my mouth slanting downwards in a dissatisfied expression, with a deep line of worry dividing my eyebrows, joining other wrinkles in a hard, irate visage; a woman who hadn't laughed for so long, who hadn't been simply happy for so long, who constantly ran and worried and was troubled, and in a rush and late, and was afraid that she was screwing up, and *knew* that she was screwing up, and couldn't see any kind of tranquility on the horizon, couldn't see any peace, couldn't see the end of the road. There weren't any firecrackers flying around me, and I wasn't carried on anyone's shoulders, and I didn't become prettier, and those who knew me didn't change their attitudes toward me. I still had to run errands and take the kids to their afternoon activities, sit down and wait for them, drive them, pick them up, ensure that the house was functioning and that there was fresh bread at home, and milk.

Nothing changed in my relationship with the world, or with myself. I was the same woman, and my life looked the same, except I found it slightly easier to spend money on shoes and I had a bit more time. And it was so confusing, so I told myself that I'd write another book. I thought that if I wrote another book, I'd be a real author, and people would really think of me as an author, and then maybe it would truly happen. Maybe then, something would move and I'd feel as though I was doing something – that I'd achieved. That I'd succeeded. So I sat down to write another book. And I returned to the exact same situation, because once again, I didn't have time. And I sat, and wrote, and erased, and sat some more, writing and erasing, gathering moments, fighting for minutes. And after several months I sat down to read it and realized that it wasn't good. I realized that nothing was going to come out of it, that I didn't have the energy, that I had nothing to give and nothing to say. And I turned off the computer. And I quit writing. Because suddenly, I realized that it didn't really matter. It held no significance whatsoever, not to anyone, not even to myself. I realized that if, after achieving my biggest dream in the world, I was still in the same place, then there really was no point in making an effort. And that was when, just when I was supposed to be happy, I shattered.

> I wanted to tell you that it warms the heart to feel from afar that there's a feminine truth, reaching and embracing through the glass walls closing in on all the mothers who want to be part of the world that's outside (you know, combining work and children), yet at the same time wanting to maintain and nurture the world within: the house, the children, the husband. That there are other women who feel and experience, and kick, and agonize, and question, and check, and fear, and rejoice, and sparkle. And I get up every day with a prayer to get through this day in one piece, to manage to be myself, and be there for them, and for him, and be smart and victorious, and right and successful, and thin and happy, with the will and strength to be all those things tomorrow as well. And the day after tomorrow. And the day after that.
>
> Daniela

I didn't understand how no one had told me. How had no one told me that this was what I should anticipate? How had no one warned me? I felt cheated. Because as I was growing up, I was promised – the world promised me, life promised me, my fucking potential promised me – that if I tried hard enough, and if I worked hard enough and fought and gave everything I had and my entire soul, and if I was kind and wonderful, then one bright day, I'd reach a place where the birds sing, and butterflies fly, and there is just peace and quiet. And I was told that it was all up to me, and I gave everything I had to get there. All my energies, everything that I had in me, just to find out that it doesn't work like that. To discover that in real life, there is no suitable compensation, there isn't reward and punishment, and things can always get worse. That after every success, you have to get up in the morning and try again. That after every vacation, you have to return home. After every pair of boots you buy, there's another shirt you want. After every pound you lose, there's a holiday rich with delicious food.

And with every cake that I ate, and every second in which I didn't do my best, I felt less successful and more like a screwup; less triumphant and more like a failure. Because despite everything I did, it was never enough. And I mainly understood that I couldn't save my little girl. Even if I were to slay all the dragons, and run to all the therapists, and even if I did everything – everything they'd tell me and recommend that I do – I wouldn't be able to save her. So I did the only thing left to do. I fell apart. Because I had hoped so much, and believed so badly, that in the end, I could only fall apart. And I knew that I no longer had any energy left. For anything. And from within this abyss into which I had been sucked, I saw her wave to me, that woman to whom

I had already said goodbye once, before what seemed to me like an entire lifetime ago; I had already said goodbye to who I was, that girl who laughed, who loved to go out, to have fun, who was interested in the world around her. And not only did I lose myself. My man lost his friend as well.

> I'm a mother to four young children who are very close in age, and it's not easy for me. I'd be grateful if you'd provide information about recommended seminars on the subject of couples therapy, and also if there's a seminar on the subject of anger management, which, unfortunately (I plead guilty and I'm racked with guilt), is part of my life because of the pressures and the intensity of numerous confrontations related to childrearing and my husband's involvement (or lack thereof) in all the fun.
>
> Hannah

And it had already been three weeks that my man and I were no longer living in the same house.

# 22

*So that two of them were not left together.*
(1 Samuel 11:11)

I went out for a drink with the girls. This time we celebrated. We sat on the bar and I told them all the details about my new job, writing a column for women in the newspaper, and we immediately proposed a toast, and everyone wished me luck, and after that we talked a bit about my situation, and then about their situations, but then the alcohol started kicking in, and we laughed a bit, and only one of us was more quiet than usual, and we loosened up, and someone else asked if we weren't supposed to be at an age where we have more desire than they do, and we laughed. Yes, that's what's written in the books, that now we're supposed to want it more than they do. And it's not that we don't want it, we concluded unanimously, it's just that at the end of the day we're already exhausted, and for sex, we almost always have to get rid of a child sleeping in our bed, and in order to give the sex its due investment, we have to dig through all the dolls and kiddy CDs in order to find the toys that we bought each other for our birthdays. And for the sexy negligee we have to wax, and in order to wear only a thong without looking ridiculous, we'd better lose a few pounds, so we decided to postpone it for tomorrow or some imaginary tomorrow that we hope will arrive someday, or a romantic vacation with just the two of us, alone, relaxed, and mellow after a good massage.

But the romantic vacation never arrives, because how will we go on a vacation without the children, when both of us work so hard and hardly spend enough time with them, and eventually, it always ends up being at some child-friendly hotel, where we run after them from one activity to the other, where we share the single bedroom with the children, and imagine what we could have been doing had we been there without them. And we imagine it alone. Each one to him or herself. Not daring to voice it out loud. And this girl talk of ours, on the bar, about sex, was so far from what it was supposed to be, wrapped up in so many layers of disappointment. Too much, not enough, he wants, I want. I'm tired. She's tired. He's tired. And even the alcohol couldn't keep at bay the bitter feeling of a missed opportunity.

When the bill arrived, we divided it in five, just like we divided the salads that we ordered and nibbled at listlessly, counting calories, counting hours of sleep, because how could we get up for work tomorrow morning, to another day in our measured lives, laden with details, in which we had lost not only the joy of sex, but almost all of our joy. And none of us talked anymore about what she'll do when she becomes a minister. Or the prime minister. Or queen.

> I'm the owner of the shop *Blue*, up north. If you ever visit the north, I'd love to have you visit my shop, which is very special (yes, I know I'm subjective, but I'm not the only one who thinks so) and I'm very proud of it. I'm also a single mother to two beautiful boys. My wet fantasy (one of several not yet realized) is that the

preoccupation with sex and sexuality will become
a legitimate and varied cultural experience. I
also founded in the city a forum for businesses
run by women. The forum provides services for
the benefit of the participants and helps out
enterprises run by women, mostly single mothers.
I'll be so happy if you ever feel like dropping
by for a cup of coffee.

Sigal

A minute before we dispersed, after everyone made sure that
I'd be fine returning to an empty house, and I hid the fact that
I wasn't, a big tear suddenly fell from the princess's eye, down
her pretty makeup-free face, in which fine wrinkles had started
etching their mark.

Surprised and frightened, we tried to ask what was going on.

The princess took a deep breath, and then said that for several
days the prince hadn't been living at home, and while wiping
away the tear with a quick movement, she added that tomorrow
a truck was coming to pick up his things. They were separating.

Everyone looked at me, expecting me to say something, and I
couldn't find anything to say; I was totally surprised. So I gathered
her into my embrace, and while she was there, the thoughts ran
through my head, crashing and contradicting, and I wondered
how I hadn't realized, how amid all the little complaints that she
had about him, about their life, about her life, the complaints
that she scattered during our meetings at the bar, and during our
conversations on the phone when she was on her way somewhere
and I was on my way to somewhere else, how I hadn't realized.
And she embraced me tightly, and I was furious at myself for
being so busy falling apart, my entire life collapsing with me,

that I hadn't seen it happening to her. And for a minute, I was angry with her, for not saying that these weren't small things, for not yelling, for not calling out for help. And her silence wasn't the only thing I was angry about. I was also angry at the ease with which she was breaking up – both of them were breaking up – their wonderful family, so successful and healthy, my dream family. And I released her from my embrace, and she tried to smile at me and it was even sadder.

And then I realized that it hadn't been easy at all. And I knew that I preferred to believe that there were fairy tales; that I preferred to believe that I was the only one who had been expelled from them, by the force of destiny and statistics.

And another tear fell, and she told me that two weeks ago, they had a fight, and at a certain moment – as it sometimes happens in the middle of a fight, when one loses control, and things come rushing out – he suddenly yelled that he doesn't deserve to live like this. And she also yelled that she doesn't deserve to live like this. And there was a silence. And he said that maybe they shouldn't live together. And she said that maybe they really shouldn't. And he slept in the living room. It wasn't something new, she said, it had already happened to them several times before when they had a fight and he preferred the sofa, but this time, after several days of not talking to each other, during which they just exchanged a word here and there about the children – when he has to pick them up, when she does, when he plans to be home from work, when she does – he went and two days ago he rented an apartment.

And we stood there, outside the bar, with our princess, the most successful girl in our group, who married the cutest guy, who had the most charming house and the prettiest children and was always the one we looked up to, who knew how to entertain, who always put so much thought into each present she bought, who never forgot an important date in our lives, be it birthday or anniversary, who produced every dinner or special event in the most perfect and glamorous manner, who was so smart and wonderful that we couldn't help but envy her occasionally, who always knew what she wanted and how things should be, and whom we loved more than anything because you couldn't not love her, and she didn't look us in the eyes and we were quiet.

And then she said that maybe it's better this way because she hasn't been happy in quite a while, and she deserves to be happy.

And we surrounded her, our beloved princess, who up until now kept the faith for us, who held on with her teeth to the fairy tale so it wouldn't just fade away, and we knew that this was the moment. The moment after happily ever after, after the end of the story. The moment that isn't mentioned in the fairy tales.

After 15 years together, and toward the end of my thirties, I feel burned out. And it hurts. The partner who lives with me is the father of my children. He's a lovely man. He's gentle, understanding, and smart. He's loving and he's all that I've got. But I'm distant. Because he forgot how to woo me. Am I the only woman who needs to feel that wonderful feeling, when your man makes you feel as though he thinks you're the most beautiful, the smartest, and the most talented woman on earth? Are there women out there who live without getting this feeling from their man and think that it's just fine?

I think I'm all right: witty, smart, and looking at me is certainly easy on the eyes. And

it's not that I need someone to tell me this;
I just need some guarantee that that's how *he*
feels. Because, at the moment, I feel like his
roommate and his partner in childrearing, and
that romance is dead.

Well, I refuse to bury it! I'm not going to the
funeral and I'll fight for its life fearlessly.
I want those butterflies in my stomach again! I
want to smile that stupid smile, for no obvious
reason, in the middle of the day. I want to feel
outrageously sexy.

Talia

And I walked with the princess to her car and asked her if she
was sure that it was really over. If they had really tried everything.

And she said that she really tried. That she tried to see the
good and ignore the bad, the difficult, but she could no longer
ignore the fact that running down the middle of the photograph
of their life, there was a scratch. A deep scratch. And for a long
time, this was what she'd been seeing when she looked at the
photo: just the scratch.

I got into my car, and I thought about the prince and the
princess and me and my man, and I tried to understand how
it happened to them. How it happened to us. And on the way I
remembered something that the prince told us one evening when
he came to watch soccer with my man, and I joined them after
the game and we chatted a bit. And I laughed at them, about how
you can put them in an armchair in front of a green screen with
little men running around, and they're blissfully happy. And the
prince said that that's the way they are, that that's what we don't
understand about them, that they don't need a lot to be happy.

"Just let us come home from work," he said, "come in the house, and have our woman smile at us. We don't need more than that. That's what we want from our woman. A smile at the end of the day."

And I laughed when the prince said that. I laughed because I knew what we want from them. How much we want from them. We want them to help us more, to spend more time with the children, to care more about the house, to spoil us, to be romantic, to initiate vacations, to listen to our troubles, to console us, to talk to us about what's bothering us and about what's bothering them, to ask for our advice, to enable us to live in financial comfort, to encourage, support, fix, buy, compliment, fulfill all our most secret wishes, to understand without words, to give without us having to ask, to know when to hug, to flirt with us, to save us, and finally, to remember to buy milk.

And sex, I asked him, what about sex?

"There's nothing less sexy than a complaining wife," he said, "and a sour, angry woman."

And I laughed again.

And the prince said that it wasn't funny.

And I said that there's no way that this is all they want, a woman who smiles.

He lowered his gaze and was quiet for a second. Then he told me, almost in a whisper, how every evening, when he gets home, the princess has some sort of complaint: that he came too late, that there's something that he didn't do, or did do but not like she wants him to, or not enough, or he forgot, and how he's discovered that before he enters the house, he stands by the front door and takes a deep breath. Before he enters his own house, which is supposed to be his sanctuary from everything out there that's so difficult, and which has become a place even more difficult than the outside world. His house has become the last place where he wants to be. And he said that he tried so hard to satisfy her, but she's always unsatisfied. Dissatisfied with him. And he just doesn't have it in him anymore, and he doesn't feel like trying, because as much as he tries, it's never enough. And he tried to make her happy, but nothing he does makes her happy. And then he said, "When your woman gives you the feeling that she's unhappy with you, that you're not good enough – when she gives you a feeling that you're a compromise, and that she's stuck with you, and she'll just have to make the best of it – you start feeling like shit. Because no one, man or woman, wants to live with someone who makes them feel like that. Makes them feel that they're not wonderful, and not great, and that they're guilty. Guilty for not being good enough." And he's tired of feeling guilty, he said. "It's not my fault that she feels like shit. I don't know why she's so unhappy."

When my husband came home, he always got a smile, a big hug, and a warm, wet kiss. I swear. After this reception and the hot dinner waiting for him, we celebrated together in the bedroom. It happened many times. It also happened that some pleasant surprises waited for him. Wine, candles in a darkened room and a half-naked woman, or a beautiful song that I sang to him. I remember only two times in our lives that I didn't welcome him when he came home. Once, I was in the middle of frying and I almost burned something, and another time when there was some issue with the children. You have no idea how angry he was with me later. You can't even imagine.

I did all this in order to keep my marriage and a husband that I loved. And not only that. I also stopped teaching; I didn't sleep during the day after night shifts. Nothing helped. There are those who get used to having it good and after a while, they no longer notice. Do men remember how to smile and tell a woman frequently how beautiful she is? Do they really see her? If they saw her, the need to "demand" pampering wouldn't arise, or that they initiate vacations or help at home, and there certainly wouldn't be any disappointment concerning the fact that they don't listen to our troubles. Because if they really saw us, all the aforementioned would happen naturally.

That's the way I was. Twenty-five years of marriage. Today, I'm forty-nine years old, a beautiful and successful woman, and I didn't know all this while I was married. And I'm starting a new life. It's hard. Almost impossible. And with the pain that came as a result of the failed relationship, a substantial and insufferable part of it was comprehending that it wasn't enough. Until this day, and perhaps forever, I'll carry this feeling of pain.

Iris

# 23

*For who knoweth what is good for man
in this life...*

(Ecclesiastes 6:12)

I came back to my empty house, and took a shower, and cleaned
my face in front of the mirror, and looked at the tightly wrapped
towel enveloping me. The sight of my unimpressive breasts, shoved
into the material, reminded me of a conversation that we had had
several months ago, after one of our friends had a boob job, and
we suddenly discovered that all of us wanted one too. That all of
us wouldn't mind lifting or filling, inflating or reducing. Because
none of us loved her own breasts. Each one of us would have been
happy to get her friend's, because they always looked better to us.
And I thought about the princess, and how I had always thought
things were better for her than for me. And how we all think the
same about someone else's body, and her work, and the amount
of money she has, and the lovely family she has. And her troubles,
which aren't as bad as our own. And then on the other hand each
of us had her own things that were much better than what other
women had. Compared to some women, we had a better body,
and a better job, and we knew how to manage our lives much
more efficiently, and we had more money, and a family that was
so much more wonderful than theirs. And our troubles were a lot
less awful than theirs.

And this was how we lived. As if in a swimming pool. Living in a swamp of comparison, with each party trying to justify itself at the expense of the other party. Comparing and feeling weaker. Comparing and feeling stronger. The size of our ass compared with Jennifer Lopez's ass; the size of our house compared to that of the neighbors, or the houses of other friends. Our success compared to male success; the success of our man compared to that of other men. We constantly see handbags more beautiful than our own, coffee tables more beautiful than ours, houses much more charming than ours, backsides and boobs more toned than ours, women who are better mothers than ourselves, women who are better mothers than our own mothers, husbands who are nicer and help more than ours, children who are better raised and better behaved than our own, families who go on trips far more successful than our trips, and it seems to us that everyone else has it easier, better, and if only we had what they have, then we'd be happy. If only we'd lose ten pounds, we'd be just as happy as that good-looking woman over there, and as adored as she is, and if we'd renovate the kitchen, then we'd entertain with so much more enjoyment; if only we had what we don't have, then we'd be happy. Because we want things to be perfect. Because we were taught not to compromise. We've internalized that compromising is surrendering; it's a concession, and we aren't willing to give up, because we deserve the best. Without the scratches.

Several months ago, I wrote to you about me and my daughter. I asked you for help concerning writing, and in the meantime, I decided that there are other things I want to do, and who knows, maybe one day I'll write about what happened to

me. In the meantime, I finished chemotherapy and
radiation, and my hair started growing in, slowly
but surely, and everyone is even complimenting me
endlessly on my short hairdo. I'm also completing
a course that I took on personal coaching, which
I started five days after I finished chemotherapy.
But as far as I'm concerned, the most important
thing I did was sign my daughter up for preschool.
I decided to muster my courage and do it, and I
consider it a dream come true. I have no idea
what I'll do with her next year, but at the moment
she's happy and so are we. And that's about it.

Sometimes I still have fears and anxieties,
but I try to repress them. Right now, I really
want to study interior decorating and change
directions in life. So thanks for everything, and
I'm also enclosing a photograph, so you can see
the face behind the words. All the best.

Yael

The prince and the princess agreed that there was no point in
unnecessary wars that would make them even more miserable,
because as it was, both of them were going through an extremely
difficult period. It was clear to them that the only important
thing was to minimize the children's pain as much as possible.
So they ended it nicely. In the agreement drawn up between
them, they agreed that the prince would take the heirs twice a
week, and every other weekend. They divided the money that
they had between them fairly, and the prince spent most of his
share on a rented apartment. "It's fine," he told her when she
asked. "I just need to paint it." And he didn't invite her to come
over and see it.

When they told the children that they were separating, the heir lowered his gaze and didn't say anything. Then he went to his room and refused to speak with them. They sat in the living room, which once belonged to both of them, and would soon belong only to her, and their hearts broke. The heir's reaction frightened both of them. The princess said that they'd have to give him some time; it was still all new to him, and it was a shock. The heiress, who was still too young to understand the significance of the entire matter, was excited by the idea of having two houses and getting a lot of new toys – because that's how they presented it to her – and she had many questions about what toys she'd get and if she'd finally get that Bratz rock singer that she'd been wanting for so long. When she heard that she would, she was satisfied and asked Daddy to tell her a bedtime story.

The princess waited in the living room while the prince tucked the heiress in, and when he left the room, he didn't sit down, but started talking to her about what he intended to take from the apartment. This itemization choked the princess, as well as his cold way of speaking, and she told him to take whatever he wanted. She knew that he wouldn't take what he didn't need because she knew him, her decent prince. And she thought that if they behaved themselves, they could remain friends. "Tomorrow morning, when you're at work, I'll come pick up my stuff," he said, and left.

The next day, she came home after he had dropped by to take some things. He took some books, and left the bookshelves with more than half of the books. He took the armchair that he loved sitting on while watching television; several CDs – more than half; two pictures that left white squares on the wall; several pots; and his side of the closet. And his side of the bathroom counter. And a few towels. She looked around and saw that everything was the same. Except there was more space. Spaces that yawned without any logical order. Several empty shelves and several full; some corners that remained as though nothing had touched them, and some corners with nothing left in them. And the princess noticed that he didn't take any bedding and didn't take clothes for the children. She thought it would be a shame for him to buy new clothes because there was enough, and she'd put together a bag of stuff and give it to him when he dropped by. She wanted to call him and tell him not to buy anything, and ask him how he was managing, and just tell him that if he thought of anything, he could always drop by and pick it up, and to remember to send the heiress to preschool with a white shirt. And then she saw that he had left his house key on the table.

And she didn't call him.

> I'm 41 years old. I was married to an army man for 20 years. From the start, I gave up on a career with the excuse that one careerist is enough at home. We always lived on air force bases – a new base every two years. In order not to lose myself, I invented a method: after organizing the house, placing the children in their respective schools, and providing my husband with extensive support in his new position, I was more than ready to find a job. Despite the extreme difficulty of convincing the employers to hire me, I always found work in large companies, filling responsible positions that weren't taught in any university, like administrative management or being a CEO's personal assistant.

I didn't forget my job as a mother for one
minute, which included volunteering to lead the
class committee, quietly, modestly, without
making a big deal out of it. And I waited for a
promotion, for a raise, for an award of excellence
and appreciation. And I also hoped that when the
time came, my dear man, who received endless
support from me, would repay me when discharged
from the army, and we'd exchange roles. But no
such luck. Thing is, when you accustom the people
surrounding you to thinking that you're in a
position of giving and that you're happy with it,
and suddenly you come out with a certain small
demand, entirely insignificant, you're stared
at with an amazed expression that seems to ask,
"What's going on?"

So my husband retired from the army and from
me (I got divorced a year ago), and two weeks
ago, my boss quit and left me jobless. After some
crazy job interviews (I've done everything apart
from bungee jumping), I decided that I'm the only
one who can help myself and I'm channeling all my
energy, my soul, my talent, and the work of my two
hands toward myself. In the last few days, I've
been calling all sorts of tax consultants and
personal coaches, have been surfing in the Career
Women's Forum and am trying to do something
independent.

Debby

The princess, who so many times had told him, *don't forget, and
bring this, and come home early, and remember what we need for
tomorrow, and it's about time, give the kids a bath, you didn't pay*

*the parking ticket and today was the last day,* wandered about the house, picked up the books that lay on the shelf and moved the remaining armchair, and didn't call to tell him. For so long, these details, and the proceedings surrounding them, were the sole source of communication between them. Between him and her. The CEO and assistant CEO of the family business. A business that they had to run efficiently. A business in which something happened every day, and that they constantly had to take care of, and act in response to, and do, and bring, and pick up, and there was work, and they needed money. An operation that slowly crushed her energies. His energies. And crushed their love. Crushed and ground their love until it became dust and all it took was a light breeze for it to blow away to kingdom come, without leaving anything behind. Just some dust. Some dust that had to be cleaned. And a towel that needed to be picked up. And a bill to be paid. And he forgot again, and she just reminded, and just mentioned, and another towel was misplaced, and another word said at the wrong minute, the wrong word, a word that couldn't be taken back. A word that left a scratch. Another scratch in their perfect family picture. If only he had tried harder. If only he had done what she asked him to, how she wanted, and how she imagined, then everything could've been so amazing. And so perfect.

She just wanted him to try harder, and she wanted him to help more, appreciate more. To love her and show her that he loved her. And to just bring her a flower to make her happy. To just make an extra effort. And he didn't. So she was angry and disappointed. Because he promised her. He promised happiness and love straight from the fairy tales, in front of all those witnesses. And he broke that promise. He – who once upon a time only wanted for her to be happy; who was willing to cross oceans and continents and slay dragons just to please her; who was willing to suffer injury and scratches just to bring her a flower; who promised her happily ever after and love forever, and together through thick and thin – promised but couldn't keep his promise. And he didn't even remember to bring the milk when she asked him to. And years had passed since he last brought her a flower, for no special reason.

I wanted to share with you a lovely farewell letter that I wrote to my sleeping beauty. "My beauty, I fell in love with you the moment I saw you that Saturday, wearing your blue dress, with a smile and eyes that told me, 'Haven't we met before?' I saw your amazing beauty and heart, so thirsty for love. I believed that through the force of my kiss, the force of me being a prince who managed to overcome all those monsters and evil witches with good intentions (or the opposite), I could sweep you up in my strong arms and carry you off on my white horse (if I'm not mistaken, a Fiat Punto) toward the horizon. My love and belief were so profound that I forgot to check whether you were a willing participant, whether you wanted to take the risk and come down from your tower – come out from behind your high, secure walls and find love with me. I thought that it was possible, but I guess that the wicked witch, or perhaps your (not-quite step-) mother did a good job, and my sword couldn't slay all the dragons surrounding you.

"The chill that blows from your lovely lips continues to send waves of frost that threaten to freeze my heart, and from a handsome prince on his white horse, I am slowly shrinking and turning into a frog. And from floor level, the swamp doesn't look so nice, and the smell isn't so good either. And suddenly there are three dwarves (not to mention a house, a mortgage, and a poodle). And you're glamorous and brilliant, successful, and prettier than ever. But I'm dead and you're dead and this is how, nowadays, the fairy tale ends. So you live in a castle with a housekeeper and a gardener, the children are brilliant, charming, and happy, but the house is dead; it's cold, and not only from outside. That's the end of the fairy tale these days, when people chase things that are insignificant in life, and lose the map that leads to the true treasure, which is the only thing that will save us (nobody ever told us that fairy tales don't end with 'happily ever after')."

Jonathan

# 24

*Thou hast put gladness in my heart...*

(Psalms 4:8)

The prince came to take the children from the princess's house. He exchanged very few words with her, and was cold, and she didn't say much either. She found it strange to part from the heirs. It was strange to spend two days with them and then one day without. And a week passed by, and then two more, and he once again picked them up and brought them back. And it hurt her to see the children moved constantly like packages, from here to there, from there to here, involving all the *bring them, take them, and I forgot and you forgot.* And the heiress couldn't get used to his house and her new bed and cried and it broke her heart and the prince's heart. And they were both worried by the heir's silence.

The prince tried to reduce the damage inflicted on the heirs, taking care to do everything that had to be done. He made sure never to run late, always to arrive on time, to come to every school party and every parents' meeting. The princess saw how all of a sudden he could leave work in the middle of the day, knew which classes the heirs had on which day, had the time to sit with the heir on his homework and with the heiress on her drawings. She saw that he could suddenly do all the things that she had yearned for him to do, all the things that she had fought for, and she couldn't understand why he didn't do it before. Why was it that when she desperately wanted his help, this partnership, this togetherness, he couldn't do it, couldn't make the effort; and now, when she no longer found it important, when it no longer mattered or helped, and she even hoped, in all honesty, that he would screw up, or forget, or run late, he could suddenly do all these things. And do them perfectly. And it angered her to discover that he could do everything, and probably could have done so all along; if he had only wanted to, he could have done these things for her when they were together, all these things he was doing now, to spite her. Now he wanted to show her what a wonderful dad he could be. What a wonderful partner he could be, although he was no longer her partner. And he wasn't willing to do it for her.

And time passed, and the heir still wasn't really talking to them, and gradually immersed himself in a hostile silence that he presented to them, and they went to consult with a psychologist. They were very worried, and extremely frightened. They sat with her and had a shared goal: to stop the heir's suffering. And they were both worried about him. No one in the world would worry about him, the princess knew, like they would. Only they, his parents. Living together or separately, it didn't matter. He's his father, and she's his mother, forever. And the psychologist asked questions about the heir, and the prince started talking about him. He told the psychologist things that she didn't even know that he knew, that she never assumed that he saw, and it surprised her. She was surprised by how many things he knew about the heir. When the psychologist asked them some more questions, they answered almost uniformly, and with the same words.

When the princess sat there, and saw how they could talk when they had one huge, common goal, a goal that they would always share, and saw how much the prince loved the heirs, how he cared, she asked herself if they really had done everything they could have to end this differently. Had they really tried everything? Maybe they had given up too quickly. Maybe *she* had given up too quickly. And she knew that perhaps she had. And that thought made her profoundly sad.

Because she knew that it was too late. She saw how he looked at her, how cold he was toward her, and she knew that he was in a different place. And the heiress had already told her, a while ago, that Daddy has a girlfriend, and that she's very nice, and that she even helped her comb her hair yesterday into two pigtails.

My sister married a man who left his wife for her. Four years have gone by and they have a son, but his half-brothers don't want to see him, and they won't acknowledge him or my sister. Her husband is frustrated because his ex-wife prevents any contact between him and his children. Perhaps someone can explain to women that even if a man is a crappy father, it's still wonderful for a child to have a father, and a woman who loves her husband will love his children if she gets a chance. All attempts to make contact have been blocked by his ex-wife. I truly understand the slighted woman, but sometimes, life is tough. Why doesn't she let her children enjoy a father who wants to be with them and loves them? How can you make women understand these consequences?

Mona

One week after that evening at the bar, I arrived at noon to pick up my son from school, and met the prince at the school gate when he was coming to pick up the heir. I asked him how he was getting by. He said that he was fine. And I told him that that was great. He looked at me crossly, and I knew that I should have said something else. So I told him that I was sorry.

And he said that he didn't understand her. He didn't understand what she wanted.

And I told him what she said about the picture and the scratch, and how she sees only the scratch, and then the children came and we said goodbye, and that we'd talk, and I knew that we wouldn't really talk again, and that the most that would happen was that we'd meet at the heirs' birthday parties, or at a parents' meeting. And each of us walked toward our cars.

And suddenly he called out to me, and we walked back toward each other.

And he said that it was only a scratch.

I didn't understand.

So he said that maybe there really was a scratch, because old things are always scratched, and he's so sorry that the princess chose to see only the scratch. She could've chosen differently. It was such a shame. Because now, he said, their picture was completely torn.

> Millions of women depress themselves, most of the time without the help of a man. It stems from our desire to succeed in everything, and to content ourselves with nothing but the best. This is how we cause ourselves, with our own two hands and through our own actions, to change from beautiful, energetic, and vivacious women into blurry, unkempt women (at least not internally, in our souls, where it counts the most). We're tired and

frustrated from once again failing to satisfy the
entire world, and we're left drained and lacking
in energy. One month ago, I made a decision: to
read books and not only to my children, to resume
exercising, to smile more, and to take a cleaning
person once a week, regardless of my pathetic
income. Since then, the house isn't cleaner (I
have two small children and my husband's teenage
girls from his first marriage), but I am free of
the burden of thinking about "When will I clean?
When will I have time to clean?" which enables me
to smile more often, and I've even finished *The
Master and Margarita* by Mikhail Bulgakov.

Naava

That evening I tucked the children in bed, and as usual, it took
ridiculously long and I started losing patience. He didn't want
to wear his pajamas and insisted on sleeping only in his ninja
costume, and she didn't want the night light, and preferred to sleep
with the overhead light on. And I counted to ten. And counted
again. And in the end, I gave up. And I passed through the house
that night to check that the windows were closed and that the
door was locked, and after I tidied up a bit, and before I went to
bed, I went into their rooms and looked at them. I looked at how
she had fallen asleep with that bright light and he with the ninja
costume, and I didn't understand what had upset me so much,
and why did I care anyway, and who said that kids have to sleep
in pajamas and in the dark, and it's just plain stupid. It's stupid
to waste this life – my only round in this crazy amusement park
of life –worrying about things running like they should. Because
there's no such thing.

I listened to the silence. And I thought about how, all this time, I had just been giving, and everyone needed something from me, and needed me, and I tried so hard to be okay, to be good, to be a good wife, a woman who takes care of everyone, who first and foremost takes care of everyone else, like I was taught. Not to think about myself. Not to take care of myself, but to take care of everyone else. To take care of my children, my husband, my parents, my friends, and my job. To make sure everything was in place, and there was food on the table. And like every good wife, I ate the leftovers. Because a good woman always sacrifices herself so that everyone else will be happy. Because a good woman doesn't say, *now it's me, now it's my turn*. She doesn't say, *today I don't feel like driving you to your after-school activities, and I don't feel like preparing food, and I don't feel like cleaning. So the house will be filthy. So my son won't go to judo this one time. So today I'll work until late and my children won't see me, and it's just one day out of 365 days a year and I'll finish my work obligations instead of complaining that I don't have enough time for anything.*

I didn't say those things. No. I was a wonderful woman, a fantastic mother, and an excellent daughter, and I gave and sacrificed. I sacrificed without asking if anyone even needed all this sacrifice. And I gave without checking if anyone even cared about all this giving. Because it was obvious that I knew what everyone needed. Because I decided that I knew what I had to give, and what my children needed, and what my husband needed, and I didn't even ask if anyone was interested whether I bought food or cooked, or whether my husband cared if the house was clean, or would rather have me rest and smile at him when he got home instead of cleaning. Whether my children even wanted all this running around and all these crazy activities, or whether they wanted a mother who would occasionally close the door, disconnect her phone, and watch a movie in bed with them. And hug them. And I didn't do that.

Instead, I struggled to make time and do and give all of myself, without anyone even asking me to, without daring to ask for help, without any pampering, without putting myself on top of my list of priorities, and I hoped and believed that one day it would happen: the day would come and everyone would understand, and bow their heads in admiration. I expected, like we all expect. Someone – the other mothers, teachers, or preferably our husbands or mothers – will notice how much we gave, and how wonderful we are, and how much we sacrificed for everyone else, and they'll call us up to the victor's stand in a celebratory ceremony, and everyone will cheer as we receive a medal. Because we really deserve it.

But no one hands out a medal, and no one invites anyone to the stand, and even if someone occasionally remembers to say thank you at some family event or celebration, even then the bitterness within remains. Because these little expressions of thanks aren't really worth the sacrifice. Yet, we continue to sacrifice and continue to expect admiration and a huge thanks. And we sacrifice and seethe, seethe and sacrifice, and become victims. Victims of our own sacrifices.

> Sometimes I think that you underrate what you have. Don't get me wrong, I don't envy you personally, but I do envy the family unit that you've created and that you don't appreciate. With all the running around, the errands, the children's chaos, and the dreams, perhaps you forgot that this is all a gift. Family and daily

problems are your biggest asset as a woman. You
have a family. I don't. The pictures smiling
at you from the living room wall when you're
eighty-five will be the familiar faces of your
grandchildren and great-grandchildren. A gift
that you can't buy with all the money in the
world. You built an empire that I will never
have. During the holidays, I watched television
and heard the neighbors singing. I desperately
yearned for a similar burden, the little fights,
the who'll-bring-what and who'll-do-the-dishes.
What you take for granted, I consider a lifetime
ambition. It isn't a lot to ask for, is it?

Maya

And I thought about what the prince had told me. And I knew
that he was right and that nothing was ever perfect, and that there
will always be scratches. He was right, because life isn't something
that can be organized according to personal will. Neither are
families, husbands, and children. Life isn't something that we
can design according to our dreams. Or according to what we
think we should have. Or deserve. And we point at them with
our unmanicured fingers and blame them. Blame them, our men,
for an unfulfilled promise, and for everything that went wrong in
our lives.

And I thought about how preoccupied I was with what I
wanted to change, and how wonderful my life could have been
had my child not been a special child. And how preoccupied I
was with how I wanted my husband to be and to behave, and
how my friends and colleagues and employers and mother
should treat me, and how I'd like everything to run. And I was

shrouded by a screen, this blinding screen of disappointment at life's imperfection, and I hadn't been happy with what I did have for so long. For so long, I had failed to see how many good things I had in my life.

> I can only recommend warmly, as a mother who ran through hospital corridors with an infant and left there shattered, don't forget those promises that you promised yourself, at least the important ones. You got a free lesson. I, who paid an unbearably high price, know how much this lesson is worth.
>
> Naomi

For example, that I love my man with all my heart.

# 25

*There came out two women,*
*and the wind was in their wings...*

(Zechariah 5:9)

That night, I knew there was no point in trying to sleep. I went to the living room and sat in the armchair in front of the silent television. The armchair that was full of stains, with its armrest in which a little thread had become unraveled a long time ago, and every person who sat in it played with it a bit, and pulled the thread this way and that, and by now there was a big hole that I repeatedly said that I'd repair, and then I said that it's simpler to buy a new armchair because it will cost more to reupholster it anyway.

I sat in my armchair, and I hated the silence. And I understood that I hadn't even seen. I understood that I had been so preoccupied with sorrow and anger, and with the small details, that I hadn't looked at the big picture. And I hadn't appreciated the fact that my man had done what he had promised to do. He had kept the most important part of the promise. In order to protect me, he had fought dragons. And I hadn't granted him even a smile. And I certainly hadn't expressed joy. In this moment of clarity I suddenly understood a number of things.

I have to stop wasting my life. I have to start separating between what is important and what isn't. To let go. Because you can't control everything anyway. I won't be able to save my daughter, even if I do devote all my time to her – my entire life, all my energies, all of myself. Because sometimes you just can't save someone. I have to stop being angry about what was, agonizing over the past and worrying about the future, because whatever will be, will be. I have to remember that the here and now is also important, and I have to enjoy it. Because *now* will never come again.

This moment can be good. And this one good moment plus another one is what happiness is made of. Because happiness is something that suddenly emerges, illuminating the sky for one second, for one moment, and then it passes. It's so easy to miss them, those tiny moments of happiness. For too many years, I let them pass without even noticing them. Without even stopping to rejoice in them.

And for the first time in years, I thought about what I wanted. Not what I wanted from other people – not what I wanted others to do, to be, to give me – but what I wanted from myself. And I wanted so many things. To find a job that I loved and give it the time and place that it deserves, instead of counting the minutes that it steals from me, because it's my time. To exercise twice a week as though exercising is one of the Ten Commandments, and to understand that it's easier and less frustrating than hating my body. To go out at least two evenings a week, and if necessary, to grab a quick nap in the afternoon. So the kids will watch more television. Big deal. To entertain casually. To understand that I don't have to prepare lavish dinners for friends who drop by during the evening, because the entire world is on a diet anyway. To throw away all the rags in my closet and leave only clothes that flatter my figure, because it won't hurt me to look good even while I'm doing stuff at home. To clean my face thoroughly every day, morning and evening, because the years are starting to show. And a good facial cream won't hurt either. To stop deliberating so much. To know that sometimes I can make mistakes and that there's nothing wrong with that. To ensure that my little girl gets the best treatment possible, and that she's happy, but to know that there will also be days when I won't be sure that I'm doing the right thing, and to understand that there's always tomorrow. To make certain that my son is happy, and that he receives all the support he needs, and to understand that I won't always be able to help him. To make sure that I remain friends with my stepson, and spend time with him, alone. To dedicate time to my wonderful parents, yet not to overly involve them in all that I'm going through because it's not healthy, for either side. To learn how to manage my time correctly. To read more and see better movies. To occasionally go away on a vacation, and enjoy it without agonizing over the fact that I committed a terrible crime against my country and abandoned my children. To drink more water. To dance at least once a month with a head jammed with alcohol. To remember that I'm allowed to say no. Nothing will happen. The worst that will happen is that someone won't like me. There will always be people who won't like me. To set boundaries on the amount of advice and criticism that I'm willing to listen to. To stop thinking that I'm the only one who can do things like they should be done. To stop saying to myself that it's simpler to do things myself than to ask someone else; it's all bullshit. To learn how to accept help gracefully. To let anyone who wants to help me, help me. To learn how to ask for help. To spend money happily on a babysitter or on a nanny, and if necessary, to buy fewer pairs of shoes. And buy only comfortable shoes. To seize opportunities. To try things and to realize that it's okay to fail. And it's okay to fall. And to stop complaining, already.

I knew it wouldn't be easy, that I would have to change myself. But considering the fact that I hadn't smiled for so long, that years had passed since I had last laughed, and that I had pretty much ruined my life, I didn't really have anything to lose.

> We women constantly need a soft, gentle, appreciative word for our insane efforts, before we're hit with scathing criticism that crushes everything we do and paints everything in a tiresome black of helplessness. So take a few minutes of kindness and tell yourself that you're wonderful, spectacular, and you're allowed to make a mistake. Are you sitting down? Hold on tight: you're human. And part of human nature is making human mistakes.
>
> Nina

After a short while, the princess started adjusting. She got used to being alone with the children; she got used to the house being empty twice a week; she got used to being without the children on the weekends that they spent with him, even though it was hard, especially on Friday evening, when she didn't make plans, and she was all alone at home, and she got used to calling the prince's house to say goodnight. It hurt, but gradually it hurt less. She even got used to that cold manner in which he spoke with her and how he never asked how she was.

And suddenly she had time. Those two days a week when the prince spent time with the children enabled her to go to her course without looking at her watch even once, to stay with her classmates and have a coffee, to set a leisurely appointment with the hairdresser, to get a manicure, pedicure, exercise, and then work in the evenings, advance, and earn money. And even though she didn't earn a lot, and even though she was slightly stressed out by the weight of the financial responsibility, she could do whatever she wanted with that money and she didn't have to answer to anyone if she occasionally splurged on a jacket. And on weekends that the heirs spent with him, she could go out until the wee hours and sleep until noon on Saturday, and one Friday, she went out with the gang from the course to celebrate that they had passed the exam and received their licenses, and she remembered how much she loves to dance, and how she loves when people look at her, and compliment her, and flirt with her. And she started surfing the net, and logged into several dating sites and registered, and looked at a few guys' pictures, but still didn't have the courage to write to anyone, let alone upload her photograph.

She stayed in touch with the young people from her course, and befriended some of her colleagues, and after a while, she started going out more, and having fun, and one morning, after a wild night of dancing and drinking, she woke up in a strange bed with someone she'd met the night before. And she felt odd. And even though she was supposed to be happy that someone wanted her after all, that someone thought she was charming in spite of everything, she felt like she'd done something wrong. Something forbidden. She was mortified and collected her things quickly and even though he offered her coffee, she didn't stay. And then she realized that she was waiting. Waiting for him to call, even though she knew that it was a relationship without a future, without a chance. And she felt uncomfortable with herself for waiting. And he didn't call.

> With the beginning of this new year, my wish for myself and for my unmarried friends is that this will be the year it happens. This year we'll find our man, the one who will ask us over dinner about our day. But this year, unlike other years, I'm deathly afraid. What if it doesn't happen?! What if he doesn't come this year either? And I'm wondering, why are so many girls searching? Some say we've become too career-oriented, yet the truth is that this is the only way to hold on to the apartment *and* the car. Others say we're too picky, but show me a girl who genuinely dreams of becoming a single mother and hearing someone hollering, "Mommy!" 24/7 without having the option to hiss between clenched teeth, "Go to Daddy." And then it hits me: maybe it's because we've become so strong, and we can use a computer all by ourselves, and manipulate data and people – maybe that's why men think they're no longer necessary. So listen up, you, I want you to know that I still crave your kind word and embrace. And I need you to kill a cockroach or two.
>
> Gabriella

And the princess realized that she didn't really want to be alone. She wanted someone she could be with. Someone who'd stand by her. A friend. And that she wasn't so good at being alone. That she felt empty, and lonely. And she put her picture on one of those sites. Some men wrote to her. Some of them were too old, others too young. Some were disgusting and wanted to talk about what she likes in bed, and one of them made her laugh. And she realized that she was waiting for his messages. Waiting eagerly.

And they decided to meet.

■ ■ ■

The sun was rising, chasing away the darkness, and I cried. And I decided. I decided that I was saying goodbye to that sad, angry, embittered woman I had become. And morning arrived and I knew that I wouldn't always succeed, and that it was a long journey, but at least I'd know that I tried. That I made an effort to be happy about the good things. That I made an effort to enjoy my only life. To really be content. Because that was the only thing that no one could do for me. Because no one is responsible for my happiness.

> It's Oren. Yael went on a vacation with her sister, to Italy. When the whole story started, her sister said that when the treatments end, she'll take her to Italy (an old dream of Yael's), and it's happening right this minute. And I'm here with my girls. Anyway, thanks for your interest. I'll tell her to be in touch when she returns.

And I called my man and I asked him out on a date that evening.

I invited him out not as an old-time couple carrying sacks of information on their backs, who know all there is to know about each other, but as a man and woman who want to get to know each other. Fifteen years had passed since I made the first move on him, and I did it again. Fortunately, he agreed to go on a date with me.

And we sat at a small table, two people in mid-life. That evening, I met a man who charmed me and made me laugh, and whom I found interesting. By chance, he was also the father of my children. And he also met a lovely woman (at least, that's what he said, and I was happy to take his word for it). A woman who was, incidentally, the mother of his children. We had a lovely evening, and I laughed a lot. And I was happy.